D0231401

Valerie Stewart and Vivian Chadwick

CHANGING TRAINS

Messages for Management from the ScotRail Challenge

DAVID & CHARLES
Newton Abbot London North Pomfret (Vt)

Photographs, graphs and statistics courtesy of British Railways Board

British Library Cataloguing in Publication Data

Stewart, Valerie
Changing trains.
1. British Rail – Management
2. Organizational change – Great Britain
I. Title II. Chadwick, Vivian
385'.068'4 HE3020.B76

ISBN 0–7153–8870–3

Photoset in Linotron Times with Syntax
by Northern Phototypesetting Co, Bolton
and Printed in Great Britain
by Billings Limited, Worcester
for David & Charles Publishers plc
Brunel House Newton Abbot Devon

Published in the United States of America
by David & Charles Inc
North Pomfret, Vermont 05053, USA

Contents

To Jeanette, who sustains

Preface

This book is about a success story: about how the railway in Scotland, run-down and under periodic threat of closure, was transformed into the most successful part of the whole network. From being a poor relation it has come to a point where other organisations, in the public and private sector, from the UK and overseas, come to learn and share the means of the transformation. In this book we write about those lessons as we see them.

Most books about management concentrate on systems and procedures, and even when they say they deal with people they ignore the real people. Here, we write about real people, and the means they used to run ScotRail during the period 1982 to 1985. They are real people, with real names; no pseudonyms to protect the innocent – or the guilty. Since that date, of course, many managers have moved and many developments have taken place within both BR and ScotRail.

Legally, ScotRail is the Scottish Region of the British Railways Board. ScotRail is a universally accepted board name, strictly speaking for the Provincial Sector services in Scotland – but within Scotland normally applied to mean "the Railway".

No new theories were evolved; but many existing theories were tried, tested, pursued, modified, or abandoned. And great help was freely given to the management team by many other industries and academics. It is a pleasure to be able to repay the debt by feeding back the ideas and actions into society and other industries.

From the descriptions in this book some people may appear to have such a combination of outstanding talents, amazing luck, and mutual support that the reader could judge the story here told to be a fluke – one he or she can never hope to see emulated in other organisations. We would say, rather, that this is a story of ordinary people doing extraordinary things, and that the lessons of the ScotRail turnaround can be followed by almost any organisation; the only sure prerequisite we know is that the top management team must be committed to the idea of skilful, planned change.

The key messages within this book, and the story of how they were implemented in practice, are six:

- Devolve authority away from Head Office towards the lowest possible level, and encourage entrepreneurial skills and risk-taking in every area except public safety.
- Vertical functionism is a disaster without horizontal interlock at all levels.
- Big organisations need systems and controls, but bureaucracy can and must be beaten.
- Strong and effective leadership, providing clear objectives, is needed at all levels; and the objectives must be achieveable, must be understood, and must be supported.
- People are the biggest asset of any business. No effort should be spared to recruit, train, and develop so as to bring out the talents of every employee. Old-fashioned barriers of sex, race, colour, status, etc., have no place in the successful organisation of tomorrow.
- When a team works successfully together the whole is greater than the sum of its parts, and the potential of each team member is enhanced because of the support and trust the members give one another.

The views we express in this book are entirely our own. In some cases they are not those held generally within our industry; so be it – we are prepared to argue our case. Responsibility for errors and omissions is, of course, our own.

We enjoyed writing this book. It was good to be able to review a success story; good to have such a clear story to tell; good to be able to share some of the pride that all of ScotRail has in its transformation. We hope that you will enjoy reading it and find herein some messages for your own organisation.

VIVIAN CHADWICK
VALERIE STEWART

1 · Making Tomorrow Better

If you haven't been to Scotland for a while, and you travel there by train, you are in for an interesting and pleasant surprise. Nearly all the stations in ScotRail have been completely rebuilt: where there were grey floors and dismal peeling paintwork before, there are now white tiles and bright colours. The plants and flowers which used to flourish on just a few stations now blossom everywhere. On the bigger stations busy shops sell all kinds of food, gifts, flowers, as well as the traditional range of books and newspapers. The architectural glories that are both a pride and a pain to the railway management (a pride because they are often strikingly beautiful, and a pain because the railway generally gets no outside help in looking after them, except recently from the Railway Heritage Trust) have been restored so that they are better presented than ever before. Stations that were once gloomy and dirty places are now sparkling, light and airy.

FIRST IMPRESSIONS

If you arrive for your tour of Scotland at Edinburgh Waverley Station, then there will be guides in tartan uniforms waiting for the train to unload. (They can't wait at the barrier any more, because the old barriers have disappeared. It used to take twenty minutes for the last passenger off a full London train to get through the barriers. Not any more.) The guides are multi-lingual. Some of them stand in a clearly marked kiosk where you can go for help if you need to know about your next train, about hotels or tourist attractions. Some of them are briefed to look out for customers who look lost and go to them and ask if they need help.

There will probably be a pipe band playing, if it's the right time of year. And flags of all nationalities displayed to welcome the many people who came through Edinburgh for the 1986

New concourse and departure board for Glasgow Central

Commonwealth Games, and for the annual Edinburgh International Festival.

Assume that you want to travel onwards from Edinburgh. You shouldn't have any trouble finding your train, because there are big clear information boards, and television screens at the front of every platform so that you know you are on the right train. Buy your ticket at the Travel Centre (all the staff in tartan uniforms, which they designed themselves) and you can get on the train any time. You don't have to queue at a barrier. If you wonder whether you're on the right train there are labels on the doors of every Inter-City train giving the destinations and calling points.

Want something to eat? If you're making the short journey between Glasgow and Edinburgh then you can be certain that on most trains someone will come through with a trolley of drinks and sandwiches.

Suppose that instead you're heading for one of the tourist destinations. In the summer time there will probably be a guide on the train – again, tartan-uniformed and multi-lingual – to point out the sights and the history, if you want. The chances are that the train will be cleaner, and more punctual, than trains elsewhere in Britain. There may be a trolley service of drinks and snacks; on longer journeys, hot meals and a buffet.

CUSTOMER RELATIONS

The staff you meet have all been trained to look after the customer – every kind of customer, not just those needing special help like disabled people, those who are hard of hearing, etc. They get a lot of commendations for efforts beyond the call of duty. It's easier to look after the customer if you feel that your management cares about you, and in the course of rebuilding the stations the staff accommodation was rebuilt too. The filthy appalling basements they had to live in are gone, replaced by bright clean quarters with television and pool tables for the inevitable waiting time between train journeys. The staff have much better communication now, so that they know what's going on in their country's own railway. And they know their senior managers – and their families – much better than ever they used to.

It all seems a long way from the Serpell Report, in 1983, in which a former member of the British Railways Board offered the opinion that there should be no railway north of Newcastle-upon-Tyne.

This book is about how the threatened Scottish Region of British Rail became ScotRail, a surviving and even prospering business. It is about the people who made it different, and the things they did. And it is about how those same practices can be used – or are being used – in the regeneration of big business elsewhere in Britain.

We ought to state very clearly at the start that we have no intention of implying that similar changes are not taking place on the rest of the railway. They are, and the team responsible for the turn-around would be the first to admit that they stole 'best possible practice' from other parts of the railway and other industries. ScotRail is worth telling as a story on its own, though, because it is such a clear story. It has boundaries of geography and time which make it possible to identify easily what the problems and solutions were. The railway boundaries correspond to the country boundaries, and this is important for some of the political issues. The nature of the competitive threat is perhaps clearer for ScotRail than for any other distinct part of the railway. And, thanks to the foresight and influence of the Chairman of the British Railways Board and some of his senior colleagues, the Scottish Region was subject to a concentration of top management talent.

The ScotRail story is not just a story about railways. It is a story about the turn-around of a business like any other business, and unlike any other business – just like any other business is. Years ago, when Valerie Stewart first worked as a consultant for British Rail, she met Colin Hogg, an outstanding man who was Regional Passenger Sales Manager for the Eastern Region. Colin, who had entered the railway from outside industry, once cast his eyes to the ceiling with the comment that: 'There are far too many people around here who like playing trains. What we have to do is to get them to like making money playing trains.' The ScotRail story is full of clear and unambiguous lessons for any manager running an organisation – particularly big organisations, service

Old cluttered concourse Glasgow Central

organisations, and organisations which are not completely in the commercial market-place. Many of the solutions which were introduced in ScotRail are the same as those being implemented in ICI, British Telecom, British Airways, the major banks and insurance companies. Many of the solutions should have been applied by some of the private sector companies who have recently taken such spectacular tumbles. This is a book about business first and railways second.

A word about ourselves. It is not easy to write about events in which you yourself were an actor, and you cannot resort to the anonymous subtlety of the third person passive when the actions needs to be identified with a particular role. The line between modesty and self-puffery is thin and subject to points failure. Vivian Chadwick is the Deputy General Manager for ScotRail, and during the time that most of the happening related in this book were taking place he was Regional Operations Manager, responsible for the day-to-day performance of the railway, with a budget of about £80 million and controlling some 8,500 staff. Valerie Stewart is an industrial psychologist who has worked with the railway as a consultant since 1975, and with ScotRail from the early days of its turnaround. This book represents our own views and is not an official or authorised version. We have shown the text to the senior managers quoted; they were asked to comment on facts, and on matters which they thought might unneccessarily offend people. Where they disagree with us, we have said so.

LEADERSHIP

It's a book about railways, and a book about business, but primarily it is a book about **people**. This is no accident. One of the characteristics of organisations entering their third stage of development (about which more later) is that **people** in all their rich variety become more important. The current concern for getting back in touch with the customer is no accident of history. Nor is the re-emergence of the charistmatic leader such as we see in someone like John Harvey-Jones of ICI; nor the renewed concerns for staff care which led to British Airways calling their regeneration programme **People First**. Survival for organisations in the last part of the twentieth century will not be a matter of systems and procedures, but of hearts and minds. So, we conclude this chapter with a tribute to the many people on

ScotRail who put their hearts and minds into making tomorrow better:

Chris Green, General Manager, and now Director, Network South East.
Jim Cornell, Deputy Manager and now General Manager.
John Boyle, Director of Public Affairs.
Peter Woods, Personnel Manager.
Ronnie MacIntyre, Regional Architect and now Architect for Network South East.
Tim Green, Regional Civil Engineer and now Deputy Director of Civil Engineering at the British Railways Board.
Robin Nelson, Regional Signal and Telecommunications Engineer.
Geoff Passey, and subsequently David Fawcett, Regional Mechanical and Electrical Engineers.
Bill Gray, and subsequently Alex Lynch, Regional Finance Managers.
3,800 Clerical, Supervisory, and Management Staff.
2,400 Footplate Staff.
1,200 Guards and Ticket Examiners.
600 Signalmen.
2,000 Technical Staff (Mechanical, Electrical & Signal Engineering).
5,000 Civil Engineering Staff.

2 · The Problem with Big Organisations

The problem with big organisations is that they are still using the solutions that helped them move from being small organisations to being big organisations. When these solutions continue to be used as the organisation gets bigger, you get bureaucracy, alienation, and loss of contact with the customer and staff. If you have ever wondered who is that strange man in an expensive car being driven through the gates of your office, only to find that he is in some way your ultimate boss; or found yourself in one of those interminable tangles about your tax return, or your telephone bill, or your medical records; or wondered why you can't get the beer or the beef or the dress out of season that you want, then you know what these things feel like. Eventually they lead to atrophy and death for the organisation unless artificial measures are employed to keep it alive. The answer to the problem is to find new solutions that will help the organisation stay viable.

BUSINESS EXPANSION

How is it that organisations usually get less efficient as they grow bigger? We need to spend a little time looking at how organisations grow in order to understand the qualitative changes which take place during the development of an organisation.

Most organisations start small. They start because someone has a bright idea and wants to put it on the market. The idea may be a new product: Letraset, the micro-computer, the Sinclair C5. Or it might involve spotting a gap in the market: Selim Zilkha did this when he saw that there was nowhere a mother could get all she needed for herself and her children under one roof, so he started *Mothercare* stores. The lady who started *Slimming* magazine saw that there were lots of people concerned to make their bodies smaller and nowhere they could read about it.

Freddie Laker saw that there was a market for cheap, no-frills flights across the Atlantic.

To get the show on the road, they start a small firm. There are some clear characteristics common to small firms. They are close to the market: they have to be, or go bust. They are therefore fast-moving. They are informal: communication is face-to-face. There are no specialist departments to look after marketing and accountancy and personnel: the boss probably mixes up gunge in the garage by day, addresses and envelopes at night, and does the books at weekends. Everybody knows everybody else (some of them are probably family anyway) and knows what's happening. Working conditions may be primitive: *Slimming* magazine was put together on a kitchen table, as where Laura Ashley's first offerings, and Hewlett and Packard really did start life in a garage.

When you ask people what it's like working in firms like this, they usually say that it's risky, thrilling, occasionally terrifying, and a lot of fun if you can stand the pace.

Unfortunately, it cannot last. A variety of different influences conspire to ensure that the situation must change. For example, the firm might expand to the point where the boss doesn't know everybody by name: then people start to complain about 'communication difficulties'. It might expand to the point where it has different branches and factories: besides the communication problems this brings, it means that the boss is now managing managers rather than managing the business. It also means that conditions in the different branches may differ, leading to problems of equity between staff. The boss may feel like selling his shares, or he may get bought out. Whatever happens he'll certainly get older and need to hand on to someone else. And there comes a time when mixing up gunge in the garage is just not enough: the boss has to go to the bank for financing a better factory, and the bank asks for organised things like cash flow forecasts, which the boss may well not have.

All this may well precipitate a crisis. The crisis is often made worse by the fact that if the firm is at all successful, other firms will have come into the market and will have profited from the pioneer's mistakes. So, just at the time when he is forced to stop doing what he does best (i.e. inventing new products) in order to concentrate on accountancy or industrial relations, the poor pioneer has to fight off competition. It's no wonder so many small firms fail; if you look at trajectories of organisational failure, you find that of the three typical flight paths to disaster two are associated with mismanaging this pioneering crisis.

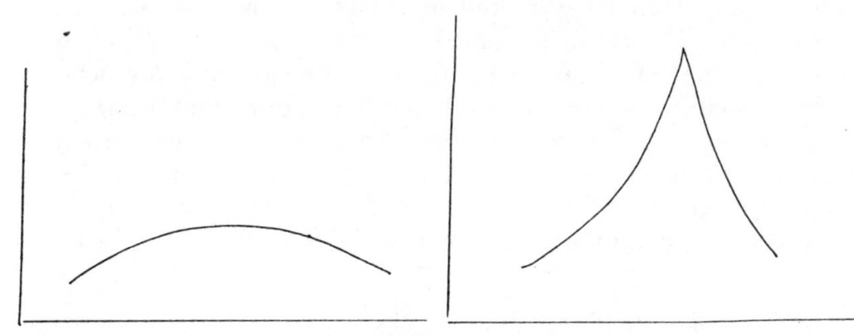

Fig 1 Trajectories of failure associated with the Pioneering Crisis

ORGANISATIONAL FAILURE

In the *first* trajectory, the firm never really makes it into profitability and dies an unnoticed death after about a year or eighteen months. You can see lots of examples of this at the Ideal Home and similar exhibitions, where scores of small firms are marketing wonderful household gadgets for carving carrots into the shape of teddy-bears, or reaming out one's drainpipes by means of a small explosive charge; they usually disappear without trace by the time of the next show. The *second* trajectory – up like a rocket and down like a stick – is associated with the firm which is initially very successful, gets into a crisis with overtrading, cash flow, or (sometimes) the law, and can't sustain itself. We saw lots of these a few years ago – Rolls Razor, IOS, various fringe banking and financial activities.

British Rail is not a small business, so why look at the problems of small businesses in a book about ScotRail? Because there is a lesson clearly visible about the way people behave in crisis, and it is this: that in times of crisis, human beings have a tendency to go back and repeat whatever formula helped them be successful yesterday. And, unfortunately, there is a time when 'more of the same' is the right thing, and times when what is wanted is completely different. If you listen to people talking about good managers, one of the things they usually say is that a good manager has a good sense of timing. Maybe part of this sense of timing is the ability to spot when yesterday's medicine becomes today's overdose.

The wrong response to the pioneering crisis is to go back and repeat what made the pioneer successful. If he was successful by inventing, then he goes and invents some more. If he was successful by personal appeal to the masses, he goes on television. If he was successful by filling a previously empty niche in the market, he tries to crowd another offering into the same niche. Sir Clive Sinclair kept inventing, when what he needed was better marketing and production. Sir Freddie Laker made some more of his 'Fly me, I'm Freddie' commercials when his airline was collapsing for lack of financial controls and forecasts.

SYSTEMS STAGE

The solution for the pioneering crisis is not more of the same medicine, but something new. What is needed is some control and system in the organisation, to bring order out of chaos, to put planning in place of reaction, to put structure in the place of uncertainty. Thus the firm that survives goes into the second stage, the *systems stage*. In this stage you have much more formality, and much more specialisation. There are aids to planning, like organisation charts, finance departments, strategic planners. There are systems for managing people more formally – job evaluation systems, performance appraisal systems, consultation systems, formalised relationships with unions and staff associations. Staff departments are introduced to take care of specialist problems like industrial relations, quality control, marketing. The differentiation between Head Office and divisions or branches starts to become visible, as various functions which would be more cost-effectively performed centrally – such as purchasing, union negotiations, relationships with big customers and suppliers – are creamed off and away from line management.

It is important, if you work in a big organisation that is getting throttled by its own bureaucracy, to remember that there was a time when the controls and systems that have now outgrown their usefulness were at one time a survival kit without which the organisation would have gone to the wall. Soon after the beginning of the systems stage the sighs of relief are almost audible, as people relax into the greater certainty and predictability that the systems give them. They know what they are responsible for, and what not. If they are line managers, they know that someone else will help with staff matters, with quality control, with marketing and distribution, so that they can get on with the job which has been assigned to them. If they are staff managers, they knew that the organisation is talking with one voice on matters of policy and procedure. It feels a lot better than the bewilderment and confusion characteristic of the pioneering crisis.

Unfortunately this too does not last. As the organisation gets bigger it begins to feel as if the organisation exists to serve the system rather than vice-versa. It becomes very difficult to take risks, because so many decisions have to go through committees. Line managers have less and less autonomy as more and more of their decisions have to go through Head Office. Staff views are heard *only* through the unions; the views of junior and middle management are heard hardly at all. Empire-building flourishes, as the specialists departments move from a role in which they help line managers achieve their objectives towards a role in which they say that such objectives shall not be achieved any other way than theirs; line managers find that they cannot get the staff they want at the time they want, or the resources they want at the price they are prepared to pay, because Head Office says No. There is a rule-book by which things are run, and it is shown to the staff and customers when they complain; and if the organisation is in even a semi-monopolistic position in the marketplace, the customers have no choice but to comply.

BUREAUCRACY

This sense of an organisation which has become slow to react, is strangled with its own bureaucracy, and like a dinosaur has to expend so much energy on just keeping itself alive that it has none to spare for putting on new growth – this sense has become fairly common of late, in many big organisations. The railway was just as prone to it as anyone else. Listen to what a design engineer had to say about his problems in buying a pocket calculator:

> 'I wanted a pocket calculator with some special functions. There was only one on the market which would do the job. It cost about £98. Despite the fact that I'm responsible for the design of millions of pounds worth of equipment I'm not allowed to spend that sort of money myself. I have to go through Central Purchasing. I wrote to Central Purchasing detailing what I wanted. They'd never bought one like this before – not surprising, since they're new on the market.

> So the chaps in Central Purchasing had a couple meetings at which my request for a £98 pocket calculator was fairly low on the agenda; but after a while they designed a form on which people above a certain level can sat whether they would like a calculator too. They have the form printed and send it out. Since I'm the only person who needs a calculator like this, the form is pretty low priority for anyone else who gets it through their mail. So it sits at the bottom of their In-Tray for a few months and then gets thrown out. Nobody in Central Purchasing is chasing it up, of course – *they* don't want the calculator, I do. Meantime, of course, I have two legitimate choices: I can stop work, or I can do the calculations much less efficiently on my existing machine. What I did was the illegitimate thing which everyone else does to get round the system: I invented four mythical purchashes within my limits of authorisation, and I nipped out and bought the thing when I needed it.'

Every organisation in the systems crisis has its calculator story – there is a delightful military example quoted in the second half of this book – an example of where the rule book which once was useful now stops people doing their jobs.

CUSTOMER CHOICE

Another characteristic of the systems crisis is the tendency to believe that the firm knows better than the customer what the customer wants. Really big firms can dictate customer choice in ways so all-encompassing as to be imperceptible: how many of us *really* would choose the present methods of personal transport, communication, entertainment, or holidays that we are offered from the limited range that the big firms put in front of us? Clever marketing ensures that the customers are softened up before a new product is launched: Ford or BMW don't bite their nails with apprehension when a new car is launched, they work on us beforehand to want it. And if the customers don't like it, they have a limited choice about what to do about it – up to a point. The market-place has started to fight back: campaigns for real ale, for addictive-free food, for safe cars, are just the tip of the iceberg. Organisations not in the market-place find that their customers start to form patients' associations, claimants' unions, users groups. These signs that the customers are forming an escape committee are ignored at the organisation's peril.

The systems crisis (for that is what it is) differs from the pioneering crisis in one important respect. The pioneering crisis is usually induced by external factors easily discernible to the boss, even if he doesn't always know what to do about them. The signs come from the bank, from the market-place, from the employees – and because of the size and informality of the firm he is close to all these. But the early signs of the systems crisis are usually spotted by people at junior and middle levels of the organisation. They are the ones who feel frustrated because the system stops them innovating or reacting as quickly as they would like. They are the ones who have to tell twenty customers a day that there's no demand for the product they are asking for. They are the ones who see the organisation losing business to smaller, nimbler competitors. And if they have no way of making their voices known, then the organisation will have to wait until the stock market loses confidence, or the good people start to leave, or some really significant customers are lost to the competition – as happened with STC only recently.

Indeed, the third trajectory of organisational failure is associated with mismanagement of the systems crisis, and looks like this:

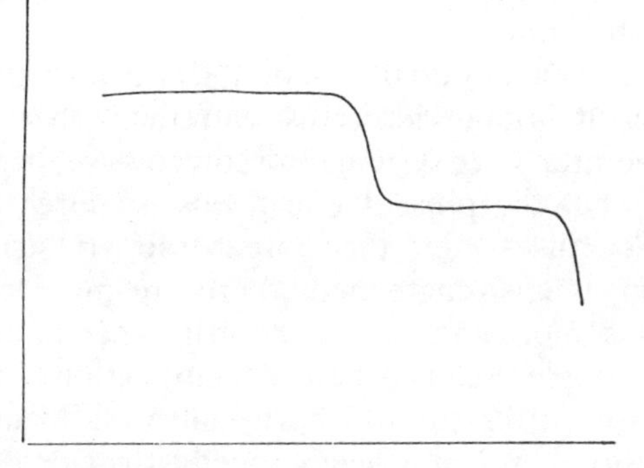

Fig 2 Trajectory of failure associated with the Systems Crisis

MISMANAGEMENT OF SYSTEMS

In this pattern a large organisation makes one or more significant mistakes, and fails to learn from it. Thus it misses the chance to rearrange its affairs; some of the good people see the writing on the wall, and leave; significant investors or customers take their money elsewhere; and the second crisis is met with dimmed vision and abraded resources. Such things have happened with

Rolls-Royce; with Imperial Group; with British Leyland; and many others. Often the organisation survives only because it is necessary to the political purposes of the government of the day, because its products are deemed necessary to the national defence or its employing capacity to the winning of a marginal seat.

If the people at the top delay until the crisis is flourishing before taking action, then they have limited options because external factors (banks; loss of good staff; mass customer desertion) impose a tight time-scale. Unfortunately one of the very symptoms of the crisis is the detachment from the customers and the junior staff which removes them from some valuable sources of information. There are other problems, too, which we shall treat in more detail later in this book: the kind of people who get drawn towards managing such organisation; the power games and ego-building which makes people reluctant to give them bad news; a preference for believing that what the forms tell them is true, when we all know that the map is not the territory; and the tendency in all big systems for intra-system goals to take priority; and the importance placed on inter-departmental fights and empire-building.

And often when they do take action, it is in line with the lesson so visible in the pioneering crisis: to repeat what made them successful before. Since systems and controls got them out of the last crisis, what the present one needs is more systems and controls. So, just when the bureaucracy is strangling the organisation, it is strengthened: there are more committees, more systems, more lines on the reporting chart, more forms to fill in, more people to consult before taking action. This takes the organisation into a disaster which is usually well-documented and little understood. When it needs speed, it is clogged. When it needs more freedom to take risks, it has less. When it needs innovation, it is given the objective of doing yesterday's task more cost-effectively.

TAKING RISKS

There could be no better example of this thinking in action than at a seminar the two of us gave to the Personnel Department of a large electronics company in late 1985. We worked with the Divisional Personnel Managers, taking them through the model of organisation growth, getting them to diagnose where their organisation fell, and they came to the conclusion (rightly, in their case) that they were well into the systems crisis and unless they took action to reduce the grip of the systems soon the organisation would be paralysed. They put together a plan, which they presented to the Personnel Director. His response was: 'If you can prove to me in advance that this plan will be 99 per cent successful, I'll give you the go-ahead.' So much for increasing risk-taking!

Ten years ago, the railway had an appalling bureaucracy, and a full-blown systems crisis. An Area Manager, who might be responsible for one major station and several minor ones, with up to 2,000 staff, could not spend more than £25 on his own authority. As a consequence, minor works just did not get done, because he had to put his small requests in front of specialist departments who had much higher priority jobs to think about. Nor could he appoint the most suitable person to a job if there was a more senior person with remotely similar experience available. Only secretaries above a certain grade could have electric typewriters, though there were plenty of other people with a heavier typing load whose letters went to the general public. Getting the right size uniform for new entrants was a constant nightmare despite repeated requests to the Clothing Committee, because bulk orders were only accepted and misfits were a low priority; so the staff rarely had full uniform, which meant that they couldn't be reprimanded for not wearing uniform, which meant that they couldn't in fairness be reprimanded for other small offences. Money could only be spent if a case could be made for significant proveable return on investment – something which sounds fine in theory, but in practice meant that money was available for resignalling schemes (which cost jobs) but not for station redevelopment because the likely gains were difficult to quantify.

More examples: the standard response to the permanent financial crisis was to cut down on staff. This meant that in order to satisfy the criterion of staff numbers an Area Manager might shut a booking office on a Sunday morning, saving £10, and see £30 worth of business walk onto the train without a ticket. Telephones, ticket clerks, and cleaners were cut down, thus making the service more difficult to sell and less attractive to use.

OVER-SPECIALISATION

Specialisation had gone from being a help to a hindrance. It was necessary to consult the highest authority before changing the light bulb in a carriage from 40W to 60W. The technical specialists broke the frontiers of science when they designed the electrical system on the Inter-City 125's, but in so doing they produced equipment which was not compatible with any other coaching stock, and thus could not be used to supplement a regular train if the original carriages were faulty or insufficient. It was very difficult to get a quick, cheap piece of equipment designed, for example to meet a sudden need for many more public address systems on trains: the technical people would rather produce something superb but late for its purpose. Another related problem, associated with specialisation becoming an end in itself rather than a service to the market-place, is that the specialists go in for constant changing and updating their designs so that they are frequently incompatible with other equipment with which they have to interface. Thus, equipment which is reliable when designed becomes unreliable because of the modifications which have been loaded onto it. The railbus, for example, which was a light-weight vehicle designed to run over rural railways, was so over-adapted during its various design stages that it finished up just about able to hold its own in an argument with a Mainline Locomotive Class 47, but unable to fulfil the purpose for which it had been designed at the time it was promised for.

Along with over-specialisation came empire-building and demarcation disputes. There were plenty of these amongst the staff: the guard who did not feel able to change a failed light bulb because that was an electrician's job; the Travel Centre clerk who would not move from his position selling Tickets in Advance (for which there was no demand at the time) to Tickets for Today (where there was a long queue and a spare position). More damaging perhaps were the demarcation disputes between managers: the refusal of the Mechanical and Electrical Engineer to let the Signal and Telecommunication Engineer do minor repairs when the introduction of radio signalling greatly reduced the need for dedicated maintenance staff; the sales training programme which was held up for six months while the manager in charge of on-the-job training and the manager in charge of off-the-job training took their tape measures to the distance between the work station and the local offices where the training was held.

In addition the railway had the problem typical of many organisations in the systems crisis, i.e. a tendency to use reorganisation as a way of solving problems. The McKinsey reorganisation which its perpetrators later admitted had been disastrous for the Health Service had its counterpart on the railway. The persistent use of structural solutions to counter functional problems made it difficult to get commitment to some genuinely necessary reorganisations later on. Like a war-time housewife turning sheets side to middle, the reorganisations redistributed the amount of material available but did nothing to improve its quality.

The strength of the bureaucracy on the railway was enhanced by the real and genuine need to be autocratic and over-controlled in matters of public safety. The railway is committed to staying the safest means of transport and this commitment is over-riding. However the need to be over-cautious on safety matter spilled over into other areas where a more entrepreneurial spirit would have been useful.

INTEGRATED STAGE

The way out of the systems crisis is another qualitative change. The organisation moves into the third stage – the *integrated* stage, in which it combines the most appropriate parts of the pioneering style and the systems style, together with new glosses and additions. As we write, not many organisations have made it into the third stage (and not all of them need to; if an organisation is still getting benefits out of an earlier stage it would be disruptive to rush ahead while there is good work to be done.). The organisations that have made it, or are in the process of making it, seem to share the following characteristics:

A move towards decentralisation and the reduction of Head Office functions.

Concomitantly greater authority given to line managers lower in the organisation, even on issues previously retained centrally.

A change in the role of Head Office from that of being a controller to being a kind of internal consultancy and tame merchant bank.

Positive attempts to increase the entrepreneurial spirit and to encourage risk-taking.

Breaking down of inter-functional barriers.

More emphasis on *leadership*, as opposed to management, and more emphasis on people generally.

A move to get back closer to the customers, find out what they want, and try to give it to them.

Re-establishing the informal links between senior managers, middle managers, junior managers, and staff, instead of relying on the formal consultation procedures to do this for them.

A concentrated programme to bust the bureaucracy wherever it may be.

A move away from **controlling** systems towards **enabling** systems, i.e. the systems becoming minimalist rather than all-encompassing, and the burden of proof shifting from that which is controlled to that which does the controlling.

There is a beautiful metaphor illustrative of the third stage organisation in the writings of Harold Nicholson and Vita Sackville-West, when they were planning the garden at Sissinghurst: their aim, they said, was to combine maximum formality of design with maximum informality of planting. Like the garden, the organisation in the integrated stage has a clear structure (and in this it differs from the pioneering stage) but within the structure the individual plants or people have a great deal of freedom; they are related one to another, but not constrained by one another.

That something as unbusinesslike as a garden should prove a metaphor for the growth of organisations is not too surprising, really, when you consider the agenda for moving an organisation into the integrated stage. Very few items on this agenda have to do with formal management techniques. Whereas the move from the pioneering crisis into the systems stage demands the introduction of a great many formal processes (and by Heavens we saw them – management by objective, PERT analysis, manpower planning, succession planning, inventory control systems, etc., etc. . . . the list goes on and on, and every one of them necessary at some stage) the move into the integrated stage is not about techniques. It is about hearts and minds. It is about trust. It is about giving up a lifetime's way of doing things, and persuading other people to do the same. The processes are very simple; what's difficult is having the bottle to use them, with nothing better to go on at first than the knowledge that what you were doing previously will no longer serve.

TRUST

Hence, the re-emergence of the charismatic manager as part of what's needed to move the organisation forward; for if you are going to say to a large group of people: 'We have to do something different; I don't know what it is yet because we are entering unexplored territory, but will you trust me that we'll get there together, somehow?' then you have to be a hell of a fellow. Fortunately, there were some around when ScotRail needed them.

3 · A Brief History of the Railway Business

The railway is commonly called a monopoly, but it has only ever been a monopoly of one form of public transport. It probably lost that monopoly after the First World War and certainly by the 1930's. Many of the railway companies at that time were heading for bankruptcy and were only saved from this fate by the rearmament prior to the Second World War.

Nationalisation on January 1st 1948 injected some public capital into the system but also froze many of the previous ambitions and objectives. For example, the Great Western Railway had expanded into air travel before the war; such broadening of the objectives of the business, which would have been a natural option for an organisation in the private sector, was forbidden. Even now the railway is only just beginning to be allowed to move into complementary forms of transport on a partnership or contractual basis.

BUSINESS OBJECTIVES

Immediately after the war the railway, like every other part of the country's infrastructure, was in survival mode. Track and rolling stock were depleted and damaged, and a spate of accidents showed how much the system had been run down. The business objectives of the railway (not that they would have been phrased like that) were very different from the present day; there was much more emphasis on freight, and the Inter-City business as we know it today hardly existed: for example, in the Harrow disaster one of the trains involved was a local train which had, as a matter of course, priority over a long-distance express.

On more than one occasion the railway had to apply to the government to have its deficit written off. This may seem like a token of permanent bad management, but railway finances are arcane and in many ways not strictly comparable with those of other businesses: for example, the railway bears the cost of its own policing. And Richard Marsh, when he was Chairman of the

British Railways Board, made the devastating comparison between the economics of road and rail transport when he complained that whenever a few new miles of motorway are opened you do not see newspaper headlines saying **Roads lose £40 million**.

Lord Beeching cut out a great deal of the network in a move that illustrated some of the real problems of railway economics. One of these problems is that the railway is supposed to achieve both a social and a business purpose, often using the same stock on the same routes. Cutting out the 'social railway' leaves isolated many rural communities, and many people who do not have access to cars (70 per cent of women in the UK still do not hold a driving licence). A second problem had to do with the fact that cutting out the branch lines coincided with a rise in car ownership and a rise in the standards of car-building. The assumption was made that once the branch lines were cut out people would drive ten miles to the nearest big station and catch

Glasgow Central old queueing area

the train. Many of them didn't; instead, having got into the car, they finished the journey by the same means of transport. Cutting out the branch lines resulted in a greater drop in usage of the trunk routes than had been predicted. A further problem was that bus substitution did not work as promised, partly because the buses ran between the now deserted railway stations rather than between city centres or the new housing estates.

COMPETITION

The freight business suffered also, as the growing motorway network made it more convenient to send many goods by road, and as heavy industry gradually declined. Grain and coal, stone and steel and aggregates, gradually became all that was substantially left of a business which had been begun with freight transport in mind – passenger transport was an afterthought. Again, the relative costing between road and rail were never fairly worked out: the Heavy Goods Vehicle licence goes only a minute proportion of the way towards paying for the total cost of the road network, while the railway bears its own costs fully; and the operator can finance the speculative purchase of a lorry (or coach) much more easily than the railway can invest in a speculative locomotive.

Few governments of any Party have been as sympathetic to the railway as many foreign governments have been to theirs. It is not simply a matter of financial investment, though the French government sank into the track for the TGV Paris–Lyons express more money than the British Railways Board receives in Public Service Obligation payment in a whole year. The consistency of purpose within and between governments has made forward planning very difficult to achieve. One of us recalls a conversation with the then Minister of Transport, outlining the reason why a sudden delay of one year in producing the promised finance results in a delay of three years before the work is reinstated. The Minister was taken step by step through the fact that the delay has to be transmitted to workshops and suppliers, invokes penalty clauses, disrupts the planning process; that the work cannot be instantly put back into the pipeline when the money comes through; and that if you get a reputation with suppliers for constantly pulling out of or postponing contracts then your orders do not get as high a priority as they otherwise might. As F. E. Smith once remarked of a judge after one of

F.E.'s expositions, the minister at the end may have been no wiser, but he was doubtless better informed.

It is probably true to say that the railway did not think of itself as a business until the 1960's, and did not start to behave like one until several years after that. One major business initiative was the introduction of the Inter-City brand name, which still carries a great deal of prestige. But the railway was operator-led, and operator-run. You can see this in many small things: the sales function effectively had the objective of shifting capacity which the operators could not fill, and for years concentrated on minimising the losses on marginal products; only lately has it moved towards the positive development of new business. Sales staff in many Travel Centres are still part of the Operating Manager's staff. Timetables were produced by the operators and have only recently had any significant input about the demands of the business. The essential material required to sell the product – public timetables, for instance – were usually in short supply because they were regarded as a cost rather than as an investment. The Regional structure which had effectively been in existence since Grouping in the 1920's, and which had been altered only slightly by successive reorganisations, placed the operators in full control – except when the Mechanical Engineers enjoyed themselves designing prestige steam locomotives.

In her diaries Barbara Castle records that as Minister of Transport she spotted the young Peter Parker and tried to get him to take the post of Chairman of the British Railways Board. This was part of a general trend to get more of the influence of private industry into the nationalised industries. Peter Parker refused to come for the money offered, because he saw that to accept the unreasonably low salary offered would be to establish a precedent, or would freeze high quality industrialists out of the management of national resources. The railway had to wait several years before it gained the benefit of his expertise, and under his leadership a number of significant changes came to be made.

Among his first actions were to try to re-establish morale amongst the railway workforce, and to try to renegotiate the contract with government so that a special payment was earmarked for the social railway and a corresponding level of service specified. Under his chairmanship there were many significant improvements in the quality of railway management and in the service – the highly successful marketing of the Inter-

City 125 train, improved rolling stock, more imaginative marketing which produced products like the Railcard. There were also some bloodily damaging industrial disputes which lost business permanently, and probably lost some sympathy at high levels in politics; and some notable failures of new products, of which the Advanced Passenger Train is the most notorious example. (The APT was a good example of product-led design; the Design Team was brought in from the aircraft industry and they brought their technology with them. They did not recognise that although aircraft travel much faster than trains, their rate of change of cant is, in fact, comparatively slow. On a railway the absolute speed is much slower but the rate of change of cant, particularly on lines like the West Coast Main Line, is exceedingly rapid. Many of the aircraft mechanisms are hydraulically activated, and so respond slowly to a change in cant; the transfer of these mechanisms to a train meant that the train was always correcting for a change in attitude that had been overtaken by three or four later ones. In conjunction with the

New travel centre Glasgow Central

high centre of gravity of the train, the cumulative effects of many such maladjustments probably lead to the psychological effect of some of the passengers feeling sick. An electrically actuated mechanism would have given a much faster response time and been far more suited to the ground environment. Also, some people say that the cant deficiency convinced passengers that they were not going around a corner but that looking at the horizon convinced them that they were.)

Sir Peter Parker was succeeded in 1983 by Bob (later Sir Robert) Reid, who made a number of significant changes to the railway organisation and purposes. One major change was the introduction of Sector Directors – effectively very senior 'brand managers' for each of the five business sectors – Freight, Parcels, Inter-City, London and South-Eastern, and Provincial Services. The Sector Directors have the responsibility for finding out what the customer wants and specifying the level of service required to meet it within certain cost parameters. The General Managers are therefore the equivalent of what in any other industry would be called production managers. This gives a three-way matrix management structure, the other part of the matrix being the technical functions. Many other organisations have found a three-way matrix difficult to sustain (particularly when it is finance-based rather than task-based) and we shall have to see what happens and what developments take place as the system settles down.

Bob Reid had a very difficult set of financial targets to achieve, and there have been other reorganisations designed to cut costs; in some cases, as happens with nearly every cost-cutting exercise, costs have been cut at the expense of greater loss of revenue. The freight business took a hammering in the 1984–85 miners' strike from which it will be difficult to recover. Isolating the Inter-City business as far as possible has meant that it could be given a target for profitability, and the contract for the social railway has continued. The political climate was interesting, to say the least; outwardly hostile to railways (the present Prime Minister, when Opposition spokeswoman on Transport, told senior railway executives that they couldn't possibly be any good otherwise they wouldn't be working for a nationalised industry) the Conservative Government had in it some thoughtful friends of the railways, and considerable investment has been authorised – for example the electrification of the East Coast Main Line. At the same time there has been deregulation of bus and coach services leading to far greater competition on some routes: the Anglo-Scottish routes and the internal Scottish Inter-City routes threatened ScotRail's business.

COMMITMENT

What's the railway like as a place to work in? It certainly gets a high degree of commitment from many of its staff and managers, quite a few of whom could command considerably higher salaries in outside industry (*pace* the politicians who think that the only possible reasonable commitment is to making money). Trying to define that elusive concept **organisation climate** is notoriously difficult, but here goes:

> The technology itself has enormous appeal. It is every small boy's dream train set, on a life-size gauge. To the inherent fascination which machines themselves have for some people is added the opportunity to manipulate them in a constantly-changing, three dimensional jigsaw.
>
> One not so obvious and more problematic consequence of this is that the railway tends to be driven from the bottom up rather than the top down. What's happening on the ground, be it with the system or the staff, easily gets middle and senior managers drawn in – contrast this with a production line, where the immediate task of producing the goods is generally left to workers and first-line management. It takes real determination for a middle manager on the railway not to get drawn in to the solution of routine problems, because no problem is routine in the sense that something exactly similar has happened before.
>
> Because the railway is a real-time, 24-hours-a-day industry, it is very easy to develop a style of management by crisis, as opposed to management by planning. If you leave things until they become a crisis you always have the exigencies of time pressure as an excuse; plus, you have control over the hindsight. You can always answer your critics by saying that they weren't there. Management by crisis has the great advantage of making you look a hero; the person who plans their activities so that crises rarely occur can by contrast easily be overlooked. And, if you don't plan, you can't fail – a plan is a hostage to fortune, whereas a crisis is an opportunity to show the great British talent for muddling through.
>
> These two factors taken together mean that on the railway a manager probably has to make more determined efforts to concentrate on long-term goals, and to get policy implemented, than he would in many other industry. Marks & Spencer can take a Board

level decision to push navy blue pleated skirts and they'll be in the stores by the end of the week. Getting a policy decision implemented on the railway means constantly pushing against the grain of the organisation; and, without the corset of the real-time operation to excuse any confinement of their horizons and their options, many managers whose jobs have long time-spans of discretion (i.e. it will take a long time before their mistakes or successes are apparent) are not as good as their counterparts in other industries at getting things done on time when the system itself does not impose a time constraint.

The industry has been contracting for many years; people have got used to low levels of investment, and to muddling along with less-than-perfect equipment. For many people this means low expectations. They can try their hardest, but can only ever succeed in maintaining their position. The motivation which in other industries would cause managers to push for expansion has been dampened by years of getting by.

Peter Parker said of the railway that 'our face is our backside', meaning that in a few other organisations would the routine consumer of the product come face-to-face with nearly everyone involved in its production, nor would they see such a large part of the production process. If you travel by air you are carefully shepherded away from sight of the pilot, the baggage handlers, the maintenance staff. If you go into a shop you do not see the warehouse staff and the cleaners. Restaurants which prepare their food before you usually have prepared well in advance for this **coup de theatre**. On the railway, though, the passengers see not only the people who sell and check the tickets, but the driver, the guard, the cleaner, the maintenance staff, and they often take anyone in uniform to be a British Rail official. It is much easier to maintain a smooth image in the eyes of the customer when you have tight control over which parts of your face you present and when.

The industrial relations scene contains some nineteenth-century practices (many of them held in place by the unions rather than the management) and the consultation system is a drama that combines the worst features of opera and cricket. It was a christening gift when the railway was nationalised, and shows many features of disabling bureaucracy: level upon level of fail-safe procedures put together with no sense that they might be needed to respond to an urgent problem. Each of the unions, but particularly ASLEF, sees its membership base being eroded as the railway contracts, and this explains some of the internecine warfare which erupts from time to time. Within the unions, the relative level of skill required to do different jobs has changed, and many jobs have been deskilled or turned into the kind of job where you are paid not for what you **do** do, but for what you **can** do when the automatic system fails.

Most personnel procedures are relatively new and unsophisticated for an organisation of its size. An updated performance appraisal system has been in place since only 1983, but it committed many of the errors which other organisations had learned their way out of years before. Selection of blue-collar staff has been unorganised and wayward. Career and succession planning happens only for very senior staff. Real manpower planning is new. Identification of staff who have potential to do more senior jobs is not practised widely and is bedevilled by a self-imposed restriction on managers to take the most senior applicant rather than search for the most suitable. Not only are the innovations in personnel policy very recent, many of them were not thought through before implementation: for example, a serious misuse of psychological tests led to the famous case of the lady who went for a job as a carriage cleaner being asked, **inter alia**, whether she would rather be a bishop or a colonel; she was puzzled, because she'd really wanted to be a carriage cleaner.

The range of talent at all grades in the organisation is probably wider than would be found in many others offering comparable pay and conditions. There are some truly superb people working in everything from the most senior to the most junior grades. The fascination with the product, often combined with family tradition, holds many people in jobs which hold little intrinsic interest. It is not uncommon to go to interview a group of six guards and find that they represent between them five hundred man-years of family service on the railway.

There is in many people a strong, mostly unspoken, commitment to the service to the nation which the railway provides. Many railwaymen get a buzz out of knowing that the nation couldn't get to work, or wouldn't get some vital supplies, without them, and they would never dream of going to work for an advertising agency or a fashion shop.

This is what it is like to work on the railway. One of the oldest industrial organisations in the country; the first ever nationally-organised industry; of national importance but a traditional butt of national jokes; struggling to hold off decline, with one hand tied behind its back; the fascination of the product sometimes interfering with the need the manage the business; sophisticated technology, poured like new wine, into the old bottle of an unsophisticated organisation.

MARKETING

The service, like all ephemeral products, is not as easy to market as baked beans or motor cars. Unused products cannot be put into store: Sydney Smith said that there should be an auction of unsold railway seats fifteen minutes before the train is due to depart. Because the fixed costs are so high, the need to even out the demand for services which would naturally peak twice a day leads to the complex fare structure. Because 'people are the product' in the sense that the customer's experience of the railway is largely influenced by the people he meets on his journey, it is impossible to maintain perfect quality control. Because the customer's time is involved in the consumption of the product a failure of the service costs the customer something for which there is no recompense – his time. When the new word-processor on which this is being written failed for the third time the despairing author could resort to playing the piano or dressmaking; not so the poor railway customer left to cool his heels when the service fails. Because the product is ephemeral, there is nothing to show for your money after you have spent it. And for many customers, commuters especially, a rail ticket is a 'grudge purchase' like razor blades, toothpaste, and getting the car serviced: something you have to buy to stay alive, but in the purchase and possession of which there can be no pleasure or pride in ownership. Anyone who tries to sell railway tickets has to live with the paradox that the British people love railways but hate British Rail.

What of ScotRail – the Scottish Region as it was then – in all this? It had hardly any money-making services, passenger or freight. It had some prime routes – Edinburgh to Glasgow, for example; the line to Aberdeen; some routes crowded with tourists in summer. It had incredibly rural routes in the far North (people in the South of England forget that the distance between Edinburgh and London is not much greater than that between Edinburgh and Wick); traffic in coal and grain and steel. Many of the stations had that grey Calvinist gloom which invited only a masochist to linger longer than was strictly necessary. The shuttle services offered by the airlines had reduced the business traffic. Unemployment was eroding the numbers who needed the railway to get to work. An excellent network of local motorways – many paid for by part-EEC funding attracted the car driver and encouraged coach competition. Local government was neutral or antipathetic to the railway. The splendid Scots tradition of producing high quality engineers continued, but many of them went South.

You could go over the river at Dundee, look at the piles of the old Tay Bridge still sticking out of the water over a century after the great disaster in which a whole train pitched into oblivion, and realise that it might only be a short time before the track you travelled on stood similarly abandoned, commemorated like Roman Roads in Ordnance Survey maps and little else.

In 1983 the Serpell report on the future of the railways was published. Sir David Serpell, who had served without publicly expressing any discontent while a member of the British Railways Board, offered little but criticism of the management of the railway. In a report where, as did the drunken man in the legend, he used statistics like a lamp-post – for support rather than illumination – he offered as a serious proposal that there should be no railway north of Newcastle. It was that bad.

We offered one horticultural analogy in the previous chapter. Here is another: 'If you want something to flower, prune it.'

4 · Time for a Change

'He's the only man I know what can change the clock. He gets 36 hours work out of 24 for himself, and he gets it out of me.'

'I've never felt that there was so much trust in us.'

'I've worked with ten General Managers, and I only ever really knew one.'

'He sends you rude letters. He once said that my station looked like something post nuclear war. You're in no doubt who the boss is.'

'It's not a delegation of work as such. It's a delegation of authority, and we respond to it.'

'Nobody **gives** anybody authority. We take it. And more besides, if we can get away with it. That's what's different.'

'I am the Area Manager of Aberdeen. I am controlling a station which the Lord Provost once describe as a disgrace to the oil capital of Europe. I set my stall out to match the standards of the excellent offices in the rest of the town, and I did it. I went in for good quality accommodation; imaginative floral displays; plenty of car parking space . . . you name it. I got my knuckles rapped, I suppose – I wasn't allowed to spend any more than three weeks.'

'Because as a manager you're now treated with respect you can pass this confidence down to the staff. I've no fears now – I'm a manager like I should be.'

'The system's been geared up for speed and accuracy. It's great.'

'There's some room for innovation, for the maverick. There's scope to be unorthodox.'

'I run one of the toughest areas in Scotland, and do you know I haven't had a single complaint about any member of my staff for over a year.'

'You've got to know the old to know the new. We've got a credibility that we never had before. It's nothing less than a railway renaissance, in the eyes of the railway staff and the public.'

CHANGE OF ATTITUDE

These are the voices of some managers in ScotRail, a few years on from the picture we painted in the previous chapter. What happened to change it? who did it?

If we were going to tell this story like a TV soap opera, we would cut to a simple but inaccurate picture of one man striding purposefully into his office, looking around him fiercely, and saying 'Things round here have got to change.' We would then have some single-handed heroics as a result of which we would cut to graphs rising, employees smiling, customers flocking, and the management equivalent of the Academy Award ceremony.

In truth, it was somewhat like this. The major changes in ScotRail date from the time when Chris Green moved to Scotland, first as Chief Operating Manager, then as Deputy General Manager, and in 1984 as General Manager. He had joined the railway as a management trainee and was 41 when he took over as GM. He is generally regarded as the person who began the revolution. But we must not give the impression that everything that went before was bad and needed to be overturned, and that everything new was good – this is patently untrue. To some extent what happened on ScotRail was a reflection of the change in climate which had started before Green became General Manager; which was affecting not only the railway but many other organisations; and which was happening also on other parts of the railway.

Nor did he accomplish it single-handed, and some of his first actions were to get on board a team of people who would be similarly innovative. We look in more detail at the way the team works in Chapter Nine.

One of the earliest issues in organisation turn-round is: how does one get some early successes in order to establish a track record and get some credibility which will allow momentum to develop. Green's strategy was to make an early attack on the problem of under-investment on the railway, and to couple this with a drive towards better customer care.

Money for investment on the railway comes from the railway's own resources but may need government consent for the manner in which it is spent. In many cases this permission is given on condition that it has to spent before the end of a given year; if there is an over-run the money cannot be carried over from one year to another. It was not uncommon in other parts of the

New Train and Station messing accommodation Glasgow Central

railway to see between a 5 per cent and 10 per cent investment under-spend at year end – money which could have been available and is no longer. The reasons for the under-spend are many and various: there may be delays in the delivery of necessary equipment, there may be a shortage of skilled staff to do the work, there may be bad planning or bad contract management. Some of the country's best-known and highest-praised private industries consistently fail to deliver to the timetable and to specification. It is a chronic problem, so chronic that manv people just got used to it and regarded it as a fact of life.

With the support of British Railways Board Headquarters, Green decided to put a massive effort into gearing up the Scottish Region to spend not only its own allocation to the full, on worthwhile projects, but every other Region's under-spend as well. He was convinced that the Board would rather hand money from one Region to another than see it effectively disappear back to the Government. This massive effort succeeded through some remarkably skilful management by the people concerned. Particularly successful was the Investment Manager's organisation, which went to work with a will when they recognised that the DGM was serious; the Civil Engineer's Department (headed by Jim Cornell, who has now taken over as General Manager on Green's departure to be Sector Director for London and South East) and the Architect's Department, under Ronnie MacIntyre, who produced under great pressure some designs showing extraordinary flair and has now followed Green to the London and South East Sector to be the architect of yet more changes.

SUCCESS

How, in an environment used to under-performing, did this massive challenge succeed? It's possible to point to a number of factors which led to success:

First, the **criteria** for investment which were set. These were two: that any investment should have a direct impact on either **customer care** or **staff care** or both. These are radically different criteria from those traditionally used for evaluating investment. The old way of justifying investment was by calculating the expected rate of financial return, and unless this could be demonstrated conclusively the investment did not go ahead.

Thus it was easy to get money for schemes that would cut jobs, or replace costly equipment with equipment that was cheaper to operate. Because it is not possible to demonstrate such a rate of return on station re-building or new staff accommodation, such improvements did not take place. However, many of these easily-evaluated investments have two things in common: they are invisible to the customers, and damaging to staff morale because of the loss of jobs. Green wanted to send a clear message to both these important groups of people that things were about to be different.

Rebuilding the stations was one very clear way of telling customers that there were changes underfoot. Starting with the major stations in Glasgow and Edinburgh, a process of transformation began. The dirty grey floors (the coffee stains penetrated to a depth of two feet in places) were replaced by white tiles. (It is a pleasure to acknowledge the contribution here of the firm of Quiligotti, who were responsible for the white-tiling on a scale, and to a standard of wear, which had never been achieved before. While GEC and Plessey are consistently late with their projects, Quiligotti never failed even the most taxing of tasks.) Paintwork was refurbished. A ScotRail identity was established using a colour scheme of red and white, with a special livery of Strathclyde Red for the Strathclyde Passenger Transport Executive area. The station signing was thoroughly re-examined. Many more shops were introduced, and floral displays in abundance.

Not only were stations refurbished, but plans made to build new stations and even new lines. Eleven new stations have been re-opened, and the Edinburgh Bathgate line re-opened to passenger traffic, though these activities happened later and not in the first flush of new activity.

Customers were thus told clearly that something new was happening. What about the other criterion for investment – that it should improve staff care?

Conditions for staff on the railway were generally appalling. The locker rooms and mess rooms were often underground: damp, badly maintained, sometimes infested with creepy-crawlies or worse. Yet they are not just used for changing before and after work; because of the way train workings are planned, train crews often have time during the working day when there is no train for them to work, and they have to sit in a filthy hole somewhere and make the best of it. Even if they have a couple of hours to wait, they are rightly forbidden to disappear to the pub as some of them would doubtless wish; though in practice some did. Lineside staff get even less; the permanent way staff, and engineers called out to attend to the track, had nowhere to relieve themselves and nowhere to wash their hands.

At the same time as stations were refurbished the staff accommodation was rebuilt. The locker rooms and mess rooms are now bright and cheerful. They have television, and pool tables (a move which caused disgruntled comments from those railway managers who did not seem to see that by making the conditions attractive you make it more likely that people will be there when you want them.). Whereas the old accommodation was frequently vandalised, the new accommodation is kept to a high standard by the staff themselves, and anybody who abuses the accommodation gets a severe ticking-off from his peers.

STANDARDS

Along with the new criteria for investment came a new emphasis on **standards**. Green and the team did two things; they insisted that instead of the old way of trying to do things on the cheap everything should be done to the highest possible standards; and they set standards in areas where no standards had existed before.

An example of **highest possible standards** is the Travel Centre in Glasgow. Lots of people, on seeing it at first, said that it couldn't possibly have been done by a railway architect, so bright and innovative was the design. There is a generous use of space in front of and behind the counters; a single-queueing system, places for people to sit; warm lighting; a colour scheme in blue and yellow, with close attention to the details of signing, posters, etc. A far cry from the old style, with its narrow doors, dismal, crowded interior, a jumble of new and old notices in various style, poor signing, the pieces of equipment scattered about or abondoned.

But it was not just the big stations that got the 'highest possible standard' treatment. Edinburgh Haymarket station, a small Georgian building which is an architectural gem, was repainted in soft pastels picked out in gold. The semi-circular entrance hall at Stirling station has a beautiful marble floor, clearly visible for the first time in years. Linlithgow has soft peach lighting to complement the colour of the bricks; greenery ascending from floor to ceiling, and a bright comic mural showing many local characters. Even the utilitarian stations were re-done in clean red brick. One visitor to ScotRail remarked: 'It's like when I drove my first Audi. You spend three or four days delighting that at last someone's got all the details right.'

Once it was clear that the highest possible standards were demanded, the Architect's department and those supporting it rose to the challenge and excelled themselves. It's no fun spending your life producing cheap and nasty solutions; the extra job satisfaction of doing the best you possibly could meant that people did better work that even they had thought possible.

In addition, standards were set in areas where ther had been none. These standards had been absent for one of two reasons: because people had not thought the function important enough to lay down standards, or because they thought it impossible to set standards.

An example of the first kind was the **Telephone Enquiry Bureau**. Traditionally the TEB was unimportant. It was the place where new starters were put to work (ignoring the fact that answering telephone enquiries about a complicated railway service is a very difficult job). It was where people were put who could not be trusted to deal with customers face-to-face. If anybody was any good, the chances were they would be promoted out of the TEB into other work, so the TEB's tended to be staffed by floating populations with little commitment to excellence and little chance of achieving it. In addition the TEB was seen as a splendid place to raid when the call came to cut down on staff; it was not seen as the shop window that it properly should be.

The new approach was to see the TEB as important and treat it as such. This meant setting out to achieve the long-ignored standards set down by the British Railways Board, for the first time, for (i) what percentage of calls should be answered within 30 seconds; (ii) what percentage of calls should receive the engaged tone, and (iii) what percentage should go unanswered. Having set these standards, the team cast around for some monitoring equipment which would give the data instantaneously, so that the supervisor could look at the picture for the past hour and see whether they were being met. And the necessary level of staffing was calculated; the staff put in place; and these resources were 'ring-fenced', i.e. managers were told that they could not divert these resources elsewhere.

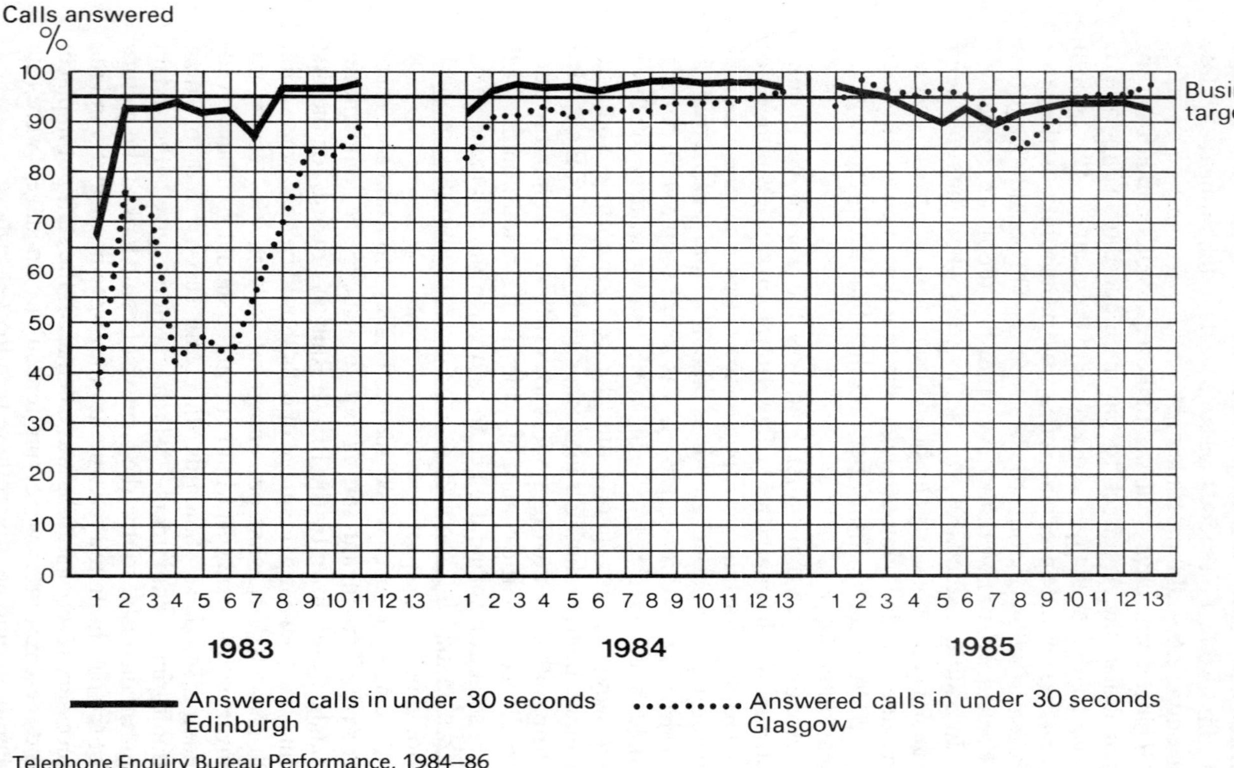

Telephone Enquiry Bureau Performance, 1984–86

The graph shows what happened when the new equipment and staff started to work: a rise up to the standards, and the standards maintained thereafter.

An example of standards being applied where it had been thought that no standards were possible was **carriage cleaning**. Engineers and technologists tend to be dismissive of the possibility of applying standards to matters they regard as 'subjective' and they are usually fairly quick to define a qualitative area as subjective. Yet we can all tell the difference between a clean carriage and a dirty one; and because something cannot be measured to two decimal places does not mean that it cannot be measured at all. A point system was developed for checking the cleanliness of each carriage, and the supervisors trained to use it. As a result, two things happened: the need for proper professional equipment became clear, and this equipment was bought (with ring-fenced money). And a system was introduced whereby anyone whose cleaning was not up to standard had to go back and do it again; previously the correction of errors had been left to anybody who was free at the time. This tightening of feedback loops proved so successful that the principle was extended into other areas: later on a determined effort was made to ensure that rolling stock was identified with particular depots and went back to the depots for routine cleaning and maintenance; it cost more money to begin with, but the pay-off in quality was worth it.

SUCCESSFUL RELATIONSHIPS

Investment in customer care; investment in staff care; setting and adhering to quality standards; these were all part of the recipe for early success. There were some other ingredients in the recipe:

Right from the start, Green made a determined attempt to really use in a positive way links with local bodies – councils, transport users' committees, Chambers of Commerce, MP's, the Scottish Office, the EEC. The previous relationships had been neutral or adversarial, by and large. With the help of John Boyle, the Region's Director of Public Affairs, who had come to the railway from the Scottish Council and Heriot Watt University where he had held a similar post, Green embarked on a programme of establishing good relationships at all levels in the community, to show them that their railway was important and to gain their commitment – and get their ideas. This programme of local liaison was so important that it gets a chapter to itself later in the book.

He also began to change the way work was planned and managed. Three important changes of style were established early on:

> Managers were given the freedom to go outside the railway to get minor works done. Previously this had been very difficult; all repairs to telephones, for example, were the responsibility of the Signal and Telecommunications Engineers; repairs to the handbasins in the washroom the responsibility of the Civil Engineer. But to these functions a faulty telephone or leaking tap is very low priority, so it tends not to get done. The Area Managers were told to go outside the railway rather than let such things go unattended. In quite a few cases this potential loss of business caused the internal technical functions to suddenly find the resources to fix the minor fault after all.
>
> Managers were held to a much more realistic time-scale. The old style was often to commit to doing work by a particular deadline in the full knowledge that enough would go wrong elsewhere in the system to minimise the likelihood of having to meet the deadline. Green's style was to get people to commit to deadlines that were realistic, and then hold them to it. One or two managers failed badly, either being over-optimistic or by permitting themselves to be pressed to deadlines they knew were unrealistic. You would be forgiven for saying a considered No – or a considered Not Just Yet – but not for making promises you could not keep.
>
> There was a new emphasis on speed of response. Green is someone who always wants it yesterday, if not sooner. One small example will illustrate: Green and some senior managers were going on an inspection tour of a refurbished station. They liked the look of the two rows of bucket seats back-to-back in the waiting room. One of the customers said that they wouldn't find them so comfortable if they had to sit in them. So they did, and found that the two rows had been placed so close together that the backs of the seats banged in to each other when you sat down. They needed separating by a few inches. Green gave the order. And checked within forty-eight hours to see that it had been carried out. And when it hadn't he raised hell.

A further priority demanding early action was Customer Care training for staff. Green asked for this initially when he was Chief Operating Manager, in 1982. The Customer Care initiatives were so important they they get the next chapter all to themselves, but let us record here that while all the Regions made a considerable effort with customer care training, it was accomplished with more speed and far more resources than some other Regions.

With all these successes, it would not be surprising to find that the ScotRail team made themselves some enemies in other parts of the railway. To some extent they did, and this is not the place to discuss such matters. But much possible envy and enmity was verted by Green's open use of the phrase **best possible practice**. He would openly and cheerfully acknowledge that he stole many of his best ideas from other parts of British Rail; from foreign railways; from outside business and industry. Plagiarism is the sincerest form of flattery, but this was not why he did it; the team were trying to establish a climate where nobody could even remember the words that are a curse on much of British industry: **Not Invented Here**.

In short, the early successes were important in themselves and for what they signalled to the Region and to the rest of the railway. There was a noticeable feeling of exhilaration, a feeling that the Region was going places. Early Railway General Managers or their equivalent were often remote or god-like figures such as the Fat Controller in the Thomas the Tank Engine books. This image had been disappearing over many generations; but by making himself and his family visible as an ordinary human being who needed their help in meeting his business objectives, Green made contact with the staff in a way that had not happened before. People knew that the G.M. had taken a big risk on their behalf, and many – not all – appreciated and responded.

5 · Customer Care

In many big organisations now there is a trend to get back on touch with the customer. In Chapter Two we showed that this was no accident; that ignoring the customer's requirements is one symptom of the systems crisis, when the organisation uses its size to regulate the customers, and becomes so preoccupied with its own internal housekeeping that it has no energy left for listening to what the customers have to say.

Getting the organisation back in touch with the customer is a many-sided process. Some organisations have tried to bring in 'customer care' through training their customer contact staff. This is not enough for a properly effective customer care programme: **real** customer care consists in getting everyone in the organisation in touch with the needs of the customer, whether or not they have direct customer contact; and in asking the question: 'How can we make sure that in this organisation decisions are taken in favour of the customer rather than the system?' Other parts of the railway stopped at customer care training, with one or two honourable exceptions; on ScotRail there was a real effort to get everybody thinking about the customer.

ScotRail cannot claim primacy in starting Customer Care training. That honour belongs to the Eastern Region. On that Region the need for better customer care became apparent when a young lady wrote a letter of complaint about a journey from Newcastle to Winchester on a Sunday. Her first problems started when the train was so late arriving at King's Cross that she was not sure whether she had missed the train from Waterloo to Winchester. She appealed for help or information to some of the station staff at King's Cross, who informed her that the railway had no obligation to get her to her destination at a particular time, and declined further contact. She had the awful choice of staying at King's Cross, where they knew about her problem, or heading for Waterloo, where they knew nothing. She chose Waterloo. There she found that her train had gone, and nobody was willing to help her, not least because she had arrived from another Region. The poor lass remembered that at a party she had met some people who lived at Teddington. She spent all her money on a ticket to a station short of Teddington (she didn't have enough for the full fare) and hoped to Heaven that there would be nobody on duty at Teddington station. She woke up her remote acquaintances, slept on their floor, and borrowed from them the money to complete the journey. Then she wrote to the railway about it.

The standard railway response in such circumstances would have been to investigate the reasons why her train was late (a process which took time) and write her a long letter explaining all the technical things which had gone wrong; perhaps explain the railway bye-laws covering the limitations of the railway's liability; perhaps offer an apology, and with a serious complaint offer a free ticket for the next journey.

Frank Paterson, the General Manager, did no such thing. He gave the file to Valerie Stewart, and asked her please to find out what kind of an organisation it was that did things like this to its customers.

What the customers used to travel in

As a result she made proposals for improving customer care, which fell into four categories: training for customer contact staff, training for non-customer contact staff, training for management, and changes in management policy. Eastern Region started, as did all the others, with training for customer contact staff.

In January 1983 Chris Green asked for customer care training for his own staff. Since then ScotRail has done more than most other Regions in the quantity, quality, and breadth of its training. We will look at how each of these was done:

CUSTOMER CARE TRAINING FOR CUSTOMER CONTACT STAFF

There are usually two items on the agenda for training customer contact staff in any industry, and the balance between the two changes as between industries. The two items are **customer contact skills** and **learning the implications**.

Training the railway staff in customer contact skills involved giving them the confidence to approach the customer without having to be asked; using public address systems; writing informative and legible notices; dealing tactfully with customers who are angry or upset; extracting and giving information on time; finding pleasant ways of giving bad news; doing difficult jobs, like asking someone for more money, in a pleasant manner. It has to be said that by no means all the staff needed this training; many of them were remarkably skilled already, but a significant proportion had either joined the grade at a time when it was not thought necessary to recruit people with customer care skills, or had moved into the grade having been made redundant from a grade where they have no customer contact. Because of this large range of skills the training was held in seminar fashion, so that the more experienced staff could teach those who needed to know.

More important – but missed out of much of the customer care training done by other organisations – is training the staff to understand the **implications for the customer** if the promised service fails to materialise as specified. Very few people go on a train journey for the sheer pleasure of it; they go because they have a purpose to accomplish. What seems to the railway to be a very small failure can seriously interfere with the customer's achievement of his journey purpose. Here are some quotes from real customers:

'I'm on flexible working hours. If my train's late I have to stay on to cover for the lost time.'

'I'm a diabetic. If the buffet service advertised isn't there, I'm in trouble. I have to carry a couple of reserve sandwiches every time I travel by train.'

'I got to the meeting late and found that someone else had taken the chair in my place. I had a series of things I wanted to accomplish at that meeting and I lost my chance.'

'This train may be only ten minutes late, but it could mean that I've lost my cross-town connection and am actually two hours late at my destination.'

'If they'd told me that the train was going to be late arriving I could have made a phone call and told the people at the other end to have lunch without me and meet me afterwards. As it was, we waited and waited and waited until it was far too late to do anything, and then the train came.'

These comments from customers were recorded, together with many others, during the preparation of one of the key elements of the customer care programme: the making of a film showing customers talking about what they expect from the railway, what happens when it goes wrong, and what the consequences are for them if things do go wrong. This kind of video has much more immediacy than any market research survey detailing what customers want under some pre-arranged set of headings. The customer video had enormous impact on the staff and managers who saw it; there was nothing there they didn't know in theory, but hearing it in the customer's own voice made it real.

Showing staff the customer video helped them realise **why** the customers got stroppy when they were not informed about a delay that was small by railway standards but potentially disastrous to the customer. It helped them realise that small amounts of information given early can stop a nasty situation developing; railway people have a tendency to wait until everything's certain, and then proudly announce a delay of precisely 59 minutes. It also helped them realise that it is not only the special customers, such as disabled or elderly people, or the badly delayed customer, who needs help; the railway has to make every customer feel special. The customer care training began by being two days long. Although it went through some difficult patches before it was completely accepted, it is now offered to all customer contact staff in a 3-day long training programme and integrated into almost all vocational training programmes.

CUSTOMER CARE TRAINING FOR NON-CUSTOMER CONTACT STAFF

There is no point training customer contact staff to be nice to the customer if the people backing them up – staff and managers – consistently make decisions which put the customer contact staff into difficult situations. It was every bit as important that the back-of-house staff – the maintenance staff, the cleaners, the signalmen, the Control and so on, realise the implications of **their** decisions on the customers and on the staff who had to deal with them.

A simple training programme for the supervisors of non customer contact staff proved successful on the few occasions that it was run. Supervisors from each function were brought together in an informal conference. Each was given a pile of cards and told to send just one message to each other function in the room, giving one specific action which that function could take to help that particular supervisor do a better job of delivering a high quality product to the customer. They then each looked at the cards which had been sent to them, and talked about them with the people who had originated them. What they learned in these sessions was how much a simple failure on their part has an impact out of all proportion further down the line. Most of them had never really visited the workplaces of the other supervisors around the table – the traditional bureaucracy prevented them from crossing the boundaries of their jobs – and so they did not see how their apparently small failing led to chaos. Because a supervisor from the Civil Engineers had probably never stood on the platform surrounded by angry customers he did not realise that an hour's over-run in releasing possess of the track could mean a couple of thousand customers clamouring for attention. Because the driver had probably never been in a signal box he did not realise that at the same time as he was calling in to find out why his train had been stopped at a signal half a dozen others were doing just the same. Because the signalman had probably never gone down a train with the guard he did not realise what it is like to walk through a train stopped in the middle of nowhere, on which every customer will ask you what is going on and you have no answer.

The lessons were hammered home later in the training session by using a case study in which every department of the railway had got involved to make the situation worse. And to make sure that this message got home, they spent the last part of the training session designing a case study for the next group to work on. Some of the best were quite appalling examples of how small errors could snowball, for example the case (taken from real life) of how what began as an error in communication between two Regional Controls finished up, with a kind of gruesome inevitability, with four train-loads of customers headed for Aviemore, complete with skis, unloaded late one night on Dunbar station where the only person on duty was a junior relief railwayman.

Not everything in the customer care training succeeded. This initiative in building teams across functional boundaries foundered on a piece of the bureaucracy that had not yet been killed: Andrew Thompson and Ian MacRae, the two trainers who did the job so ably, were on the staff of the Regional Passenger Manager, and so could not be released to train the Operating Manager's staff.

CUSTOMER CARE CONFERENCES

ScotRail has held a number of Customer Care conferences where representatives of the whole business meet to analyse the problems and come up with solutions. There is a great danger that such conferences can become talking shops, long on analysis and short on problem-solving. And the problems analysed at such events are usually not those within the grasp of the people there to solve; they tend to be the great issues over which nobody has any control.

The ScotRail conferences set out to be different from the usual talking shop, and they have got progressively more so. At the first one there was a speaker from Marks & Spencer (particularly enlightening on the subject of bureaucracy and how to avoid it) and the Chairman of the Transport Users' Consultative Committee, Colonel Bill Dalziel, with some of the TUCC members. There was a prize offered for the best problem analysis and solution, with the strong caveat that the solutions had to be implementable by the people present at the Conference.

From that first conference sprang a number of smaller, Area-based conferences, largely self-organised and composed of all grades of staff, from all departments. A conscious effort was made to stick to the rule that the outcomes must be practical and linked to the business objectives. And the reports were often written by people low down in the hierarchy but full of ideas – drivers, guards, etc. The important thing is that the reports were eagerly awaited by top management and they were read. Senior managers often referred to them and used them in choosing priorities. Contrast this with another Region's customer care training programme, where eighteen months after the staff had been asked for ideas on improving the service the ideas had not even been acknowledged, let alone undertstood.

GETTING MANAGERS IN TOUCH WITH THE CUSTOMER

In many ways this is the most difficult and unremitting task in the whole customer care mission. Customer contact staff are usually close to the needs of the customer – they can't help it. But a manager who is several levels remote from contact with the customer may do his job to the best of his abilities and find that he is drawn into putting the needs of the system above those of the customer.

Some of the actions taken to get managers back in touch with the customer are best described in the chapter on busting the bureaucracy, because the organisation needs to undergo a complete change of climate before it is properly user-oriented. However, we can pick out just a few of the many things that we done to make it easier for senior and middle managers, and managers of technical functions, to get back to the customer:

One of the first actions, important more for what it signified than in itself, was Chris Green's first day as General Manager. He took a phone-in on Radio Clyde and asked for the names and addresses of all those callers who had failed to get through. Then he distributed them throughout his senior managers, from every function, and told then that one of the day's tasks was to ring up these people, find out what they wanted, and attend to them. One wonders who was more surprised: the callers, or the managers.

A second action was the appointment of a Customer Care manager in Head Office. This is a potentially dangerous move, because there can be a tendency for other managers to think they don't have to bother about customer care because someone central is taking care of it. The Customer Care manager becomes an umbrella or a road-sweeper. If he is to be part of the team, much depends on the power and personality of the customer care manager and the role he is given in the organisation. If he becomes the person who answers complaints, and little else, then the battle is lost before it is started. To be effective, a customer complaints manager must have the power to be proactive, to spot trends and bring them to people's attention, to help release resources. He must be the kind of person whom the staff find easy to talk to when they can't get answers to their own problems and queries.

The person appointed, Ron Smith, was and is not an office-bound creature content to apologise for yesterday's mistakes. He has taken a hand in all sorts of projects, from training staff through to management initiatives. He was once an Area Manager, so he knows the problems on the ground, and people find him easy to talk to. He is one of those who never stops thinking about customers: catching a sleeper, he'll talk to the attendants about customers and customer care. It's one sign of his effectiveness that he spends more time dealing with staff and managers than with customers themselves; another sign is that the staff and managers value his input and see him as part of them.

AREA BUSINESS GROUPS

A third initiative to bring managers in touch with the customer was the introduction of **Area Business Groups**. These were begun in order to bring together at Area level all the functions under the leadership of the Area Manager. The Area Business Groups try as far as possible to run their own area as a profit centre. This forces the functional specialists – the engineers, technical staff, administrative staff – to look more closely at the needs of their own Area and how those needs can be served cost-effectively. Whereas previously an engineer might carry out a project to a specification or time-scale laid down at ScotRail House or the British Railways Board, now he would have to consider it in the light of whether it met the needs of his own Area and could be funded wholly or in part by his Area.

There is no point creating new structures unless they have a mission to accomplish and some resources available. The Business Groups were given much more freedom in decision-taking, and the Area Managers allowed to spend more money. The amount they could spend without senior management sanction went up from £25 to seven tranches of £10,000. It was made clear to them that they were trusted to act independently and not come asking for permission to spend their own money.

We go into the philosophy behind decentralisation in Chapter Six. For the moment, two results of the move to Area Business Groups are worth noting. The ABG at Inverness, faced with a crisis in coach competition, spotted that an early morning High Speed Train could be made to start its journey at Elgin, and pick up some more trade. They took the decision and then told people they'd taken it, rather than asking for permission. Chris Green later remarked, truthfully, that in pre-reformation days on the railway this would have got them fired rather than commended. And the ABG at Edinburgh put up a proposal for spending about £97,000 on improvements for customer care; it got a Yes from the General Manager and it got it within three days.

This speed of reaction is important. The previous style on the railway would have been to wait a long time and then subject the proposal to a long series of modifications. The new style – a quick and unambiguous response to a good idea – sent a message round the system: 'Here, this man's serious; don't fool about with him and he won't fool about with you.' Green did something similar the week that the Glasgow Telephone Enquiry Bureau hit its performance targets for the first time; at the end of the week he went down to present a case of wine to the staff. He himself would probably say of the first example that there is no point in wasting time delaying a good idea, and of the second that it was a courtesy to people who had done a good job. But there's no doubt that if you want to convince people that there has been a change in management style, then hitting the gossip network works far better than any series of conferences or management briefs.

Yet another way in which managers were brought in touch with the customer was the use of customer care audits. These were introduced by Ian Fowler, the Passenger Terminals Manager at the British Railways Board. An innovative and enthusiastic manager, he had the idea of getting teams of managers to visit other Regions **as customers**. This was a novelty. Usually when managers wish to travel they use their pass, and their secretary gives them an itinerary. So they miss the routine agonies which other mortals suffer: they do not have to struggle through the time-table or queue for a ticket. They probably go first class. Their pass identifies them to the staff, which means that they often get special treatment and the staff will perhaps perform that

New interiors, standard-class coaching stock

extra bit better. Their own knowledge of the railway means that they can often tell when something's going wrong, and guess what it is and how long it will be before it is put to rights. In other words, a railway manager has an easier journey because he's shielded from some parts of the customers' experience and has special knowledge to remove some of the worry when things go wrong.

Going on a customer care audit, the managers have to behave as if they were ordinary passengers. They look up their own timetables; they buy their own tickets. They use the loos and the waiting rooms. They go second-class. Sometimes they travel at weekends. And they visit parts of the railway with which they are unfamiliar, so that as far as possible they have no local knowledge to help them understand what's going on. Perhaps this seems such an obvious move that it is nothing to make a fuss about, but it was not so obvious to at least one manager from the Eastern Region, who when invited to go on an audit visit complained that he could see no point in buying himself a ticket when he had a pass and a secretary to take care of such things.

They have a check-list of things to look for, so as to get some standardisation between different teams of managers. And they come up with many, many insights into the way the railway looks to someone who is using the train for maybe the first time, or who has not got the benefit of familiarity with their own small part of the system. ScotRail learned a lot about the things that needed pulling up to standard; of course, the audit system only works if the managers audited don't know that the team is coming, and treat the outcome as a learning exercise rather than criticism.

One move towards improving customer care caused some raised eyebrows. The introduction of **service excellence awards** for staff who had been seen to give special service to the customer went against many of the established traditions. Selected managers were given books of vouchers for the sum of £10, which they could issue to anyone they saw giving outstanding service. The vouchers could be cashed at the end of the person's shift. Of course, this is a way of giving instant appreciation of good work; it is especially useful in an organisation where people get instant complaints for poor performance but little instant reward for good work and it hits the gossip network. But it caused the bureaucrats a few raised eyebrows: how could managers be trusted to hand them out equitably? Wouldn't there be all sorts of problems with fraud? Needless to say, these fears were unfounded.

These are just a few of the pieces in the mosaic which together add up to getting the whole organisation facing in the direction of the customer. Some of the pieces are small and unremitting, such as going through all the written material produced and replacing **passenger** by **customer** throughout, and drilling the word **passenger** out of one's speech unless it is needed to distinguish warm bodies from coal and parcels. Some pieces are larger: looking afresh at every management appointment to make sure that the person appointed thinks customer, or changing the criteria for the appointment of staff and supervisors to reflect this new priority. The objective is to have caring for the customer as a non-negotiable thread running through every decision taken, every action performed; not to have it tacked on as an optional extra to be satisfied by training the customer contact staff.

6 · Busting the Bureaucracy

Vivian Chadwick, when he was Regional Operations Manager for ScotRail, wrote 'busting the bureaucracy' into the Regional Operating Plan. We can safely predict that the task will not be finished by the end of the decade.

We have already given some illustrations of the way the bureaucracy on the railway is unhelpful. The railway was over-centralised; the revenue budget and the expenditure budget met for the first time at General Manager level. Interlocking committees made it almost impossible to get anything done quickly. Paperwork abounded, and more of it was produced to justify one's position than to advance matters forward. Data were collected on things that didn't matter (for example you could find out months after the event whether a particular seat on a train had been reserved) and were not collected about things that did matter (for example the use of the computerised reservation system as a way of predicting likely overloaded trains in time to do something about it).

The centralisation of some services at the British Railways Board level made them more of a hindrance than a help. A national marketing initiative designed to attract mothers with children to go on a day out was begun when the schools in England were just going on holiday and the schools in Scotland just going back. Centralisation of industrial relations reduced the opportunity to take local initiatives; hence the rest of the railway has a system whereby disciplinary hearings for staff are taken at Area Manager level, except in ScotRail and the Eastern Region where they have now been delegated to the worker's immediate manager, with the intention of ultimately being at supervisor level, where they belong. Centralisation of personnel services produces rules and regulations which are unhelpful in local situations; more importantly, when your proposals have to be bargained for at central rather than local level they suffer a change in priorities. Something you would never have given away yourself because it is number one on your own agenda becomes a bargaining counter, to be disposed of for a price, when it is only one of a number of agenda items for a central person negotiating with the union.

Even the nationally-agreed rate of pay, which has many things to commend it, becomes a handicap when it prevents the southern parts of the railway from recruiting good people because it's too low, and prevents ScotRail offering some employment in places like Inverness because it's too high.

There was over-specialisation (the Central Design office at Derby had a full-time loo seat specialist). Not surprisingly, these people try to gather work to themselves rather than see other people encroach on their specialities. This often leads to equipment which is over-engineered for its purpose, and sometimes late, when something simple and robust would do.

An overdose of bureaucracy lets the iron enter the soul. People come to believe that anything they suggest will be turned down, so they stop making suggestions. Many of the initiatives which ScotRail have taken are open to the rest of the railway, but somehow don't get done because the prevailing superstition is that whatever it is, it can't be done. And in an organisation like the railway, which is committed to safety and has to be autocratic about safety, one has the problem of balancing the demolition of the bureaucracy against the maintenance of a necessarily autocratic attitude towards safety.

What does **busting the bureaucracy** look like in practice? In no particular order of importance or chronological order, (you can't put an order to it; it's an unremitting task, like customer care), here are some of the management principles employed:

BREAK UNHELPFUL RULES

And damn the consequences. For example, the situation with uniforms was consistently appalling; they were late, ill-fitting, cheap, and unattractive. Staff in some grades were ordered to wear uniforms, but often could not because the uniforms were not there or did not fit. When it became apparent that despite repeated representations to the Clothing Committee nothing was being done to improve the uniform situation, the General Manager gave the order to buy routine items of clothing at Marks & Spencer. Even then, problems remained with specialist uniforms; the Travel Centre uniforms were particularly nasty, and some Travel Centres were notorious as places where uniform was optional. At Glasgow Central Travel Centre the staff were given the authority to design their own uniforms; they produced an attractive tartan design. The uniforms cost £200 each. The Finance Manager's reaction: 'How can we afford that?' The General Manager's reaction: 'Do they look good?' Now all Travel Centres have their own uniform, and you are unlikely to find anyone not looking smartly turned out. It is a small price to pay, but it meant breaking the rules.

DON'T ISSUE RULES, ISSUE PRINCIPLES

Of course an organisation needs some sense of order to make it a coherent whole. But there is a world of difference between dictating to people what they should do and giving them guidelines within which to use their discretion. For example, in the old days there would have been strict regulations governing the coverage of shifts in the event of someone being sick. This would mean in some cases that too many people were there, because the rules said so, and sometimes not enough. Now the supervisor is told to use his discretion to man the shift in order to meet the demands of the work; he does not have a rule-book dictating his every decision for him, but he is clear about what he is supposed to achieve.

DECENTRALISE CONTROL

We have already given some examples of how the power of the centre was reduced – the Area Business Groups, the increased spending powers of Area Managers, the pushing of the disciplinary process down to supervisors, etc. Another example concerns the settlement of small claims from customers who have a complaint about the railway, or want a refund on unused tickets. Previously these would have had to go all the way up to Head Office and back, causing a delay of several weeks – no small matter for a customer who is out of pocket for a genuine reason. Now Area Managers have authority to settle refunds on the spot, and to settle claims of up to £100 in cases of, say, damage to personal clothing. Areas now have responsibility for supervising their Heavy Cleaning Squads – how on earth could such local needs be overseen from Head Office? and for many personnel functions such as redundancy payments and retirement on grounds of ill health.

TRUST

People respond better when they feel that they are trusted. Of course, one does not trust someone to risk £100 million without some overseeing, but trust in the everyday decisions is important. When the Area Managers were allowed to spend their tranches of £10,000, they did not blow the lot on stupid projects as some people had predicted. One thought long and hard before buying a top-notch electric typewriter for use in the Travel Centre; people of that grade were not normally allowed access to typewriters, but the AM took the view that letters to the public should be well-presented. The Training Department wanted some equipment for use in the YTS scheme. Peter Farrell, the training officer concerned, rang up his boss, made his case, and got it. 'You could never have done that before,' he said. 'You would have had to submit proposals and papers, and if there was anything cheap and nasty by way of substitute that's what you'd get. It makes me feel that they trust me to know what I want to do my job.' And, of course, he's unlikely to abuse that trust, because he wouldn't want to let down the boss who trusts him or the team who also have claim to those resources.

Trust also means relying on people to do things rather than confirming everything in writing and then checking and re-checking. The ScotRail climate is noticeably more informal than other parts of the railway; people ring each other up or pop in to see each other rather than communicating formally or through committees. Everybody being in one location has major advantages for personal relationships and team building, unlike the less fortunate London Midland Region where the Headquarters Team is split between Birmingham, Crewe, and Derby.

Trust does not mean abandoning all control; often it means changing the **form** that the control takes. Instead of trying to collect masses of data on everything (which inevitably clogs up the system with reports which have the status of archaeology by the time they are read) it is better to take micrometer slices through the organisation and then, if one finds something wrong, insisting that it is corrected quickly.

Trust means being prepared to believe the best of other people until proved otherwise. It means representing the viewpoints of other people, even when they're different, if they're not present at a meeting. There is very little internal bickering in most

ScotRail teams – much less than in many similar large organisations.

George Lafferty, a participant on an Ullswater course (about which more in Chapter Seven) defined trust as **total reliance under severe threat**. It's not a bad definition for a commodity that is usually in short supply in bureaucracies. The best illustration of trust we can offer is the incident of the Queen arriving at Glasgow Central. The announcer on the public address system welcomed Her Majesty to ScotRail and asked the crowd to give her a good Scottish welcome. The Queen looked up and beamed delightedly. And who made the announcement? Not some senior manager reading from a prepared script, with an understudy on stand-by; no, it was the regular announcer, a 19-year-old girl who'd been trusted to give the welcome in her own way.

HAVE FUN

Bureaucracy-busting can and ought to be fun at times. There's no sound so delightful as that of a stuffed shirt exploding. Viv Chadwick once issued a Works Order for a dot-matrix display to go on the side of locomotives; this in a time when there were lots of locomotive-naming ceremonies outstanding, and the dot-matrix display would enable any locomotive to carry any name for the day. Despite the fact that the order was dated April 1st, it was solemnly taken on board by most of the other functions. Seriously, though, Robert Townsend said that if you're not in business for fun or profit, what the hell are you doing here? and the ScotRail style is to try to give people a bit of both – as happened when all the staff associated with opening the Bathgate Service at Easter 1986 received a small Easter Egg as a thank-you for their hard work in getting the service ready.

ENABLING SYSTEMS

A key feature of an organisation that has busted its bureaucracy is that it moves from having **controlling** systems to **enabling** systems. A controlling system is all-encompassing; it puts the burden of proof upon the person who want to break out of the system; and it thereby ensures that the over-riding goal is that everybody performs to a minimum standard rather than some people excelling. An enabling system, by contrast, tries to empower people to do their jobs better; so it controls only the bare minimum of what it needs to control; places the burden of proof on the system rather than the person trying to break out of it – it is up to the system to demonstrate why he shouldn't be allowed to do what he wants to do, rather than the other way around. Enabling systems thus make for inventiveness, speed, and excellence. Donnie MacLeod, the Area Manager at Glasgow Central, relates that 25 years ago when he was a Class 2 District Inspector in the Inverness Area, he was asked for suggestions to reduce working costs. He submitted a 10-page document for introducing what he called 'purser trains', i.e. trains on which the guard would act as a fare collector, thus eliminating the need to have people on the stations selling tickets. Instead of a thank-you he was requested to report to the Chief District Inspector and informed that the Line Suerintendent thought his proposals heretical. It's different now: ScotRail was the first Region to introduce Open Stations, which is what Donnie MacLeod was advocating so many years ago. Briefing Groups are used so that managers can communicate with staff about what they want to achieve rather than what's gone wrong. Area Managers have responsibility to recruit staff to an overall agreed number – the number itself is agreed with ScotRail House, but the mix of staff is left to the Area Manager's discretion.

PERSONAL AUTHORITY AND VISIBILITY

An essential part of busting the bureaucracy is a move from prescribing what people will do to trusting and expecting them to do their best. You cannot feel loyalty to a management manual, nor to a photograph you see in a newsletter from time to time. People need to know their boss personally if they are to feel that he will back them up when they try something new. The top team on ScotRail are perhaps more visible to the people on the ground than ever before. It's difficult to say how this is done without sounding pious, because so much is that ordinary human touch which has been debased by generations of politicians and place-seekers; but it means a senior manager drinking pints with the guards and railmen, and enjoying it because they're teaching him things he didn't know; the senior manager's wife admitting to the travel clerk that her teenage kids are a problem too. It means the General Manager and his family wandering on to the station in Sunday casuals, talking to the staff. And it means, for the senior managers, being prepared to let their people know that they're going into bat for them; in the 1985 guards' dispute, when the British Rail presence on the media was low-key, many people in the South of England told Valerie Stewart that 'the only British Rail manager I can remember was that chap from Scotland with the charts behind him.' It's the Mountbattens and MacArthurs who bust the bureaucracy, not the Portals and the Ismays; and they do this by being able to sit on a lorry wheel and talk to the troops, and stick their medals on their chest and put on a show – either way, they get people committed enough to want to die for them.

CHOOSE YOUR PEOPLE

Certain people are drawn towards being bureaucratic, and others hate it. One of the problems with big organisations is that they suck in the bureaucrats; the bureaucrats then rise to a level in the organisation where they are controlling the systems; and everything freezes over. There is more on this in Chapter Nine on Teamwork. So the long-term strategy for busting the bureaucracy involves getting people who are immunised against bureaucracy at key points in the organisation. In ScotRail an unusual strategy was adopted: that of a pincer movement directed towards the middle from the top and the bottom.

One way in which organisations try to change their climate is from the top downwards. In this strategy, top management sends a message to middle managers, with instructions to do things differently. After a while they send down a test message to see if things are being done differently. Since these things usually take longer than senior managers expect, and since middle managers are more likely to send such a message downwards than to act on it themselves, the test message gets a negative response. So top management sends down a second message, which gets confused with the first . . . and so on, until the poor people at the bottom don't know what to do and the whole thing becomes a paper exercise.

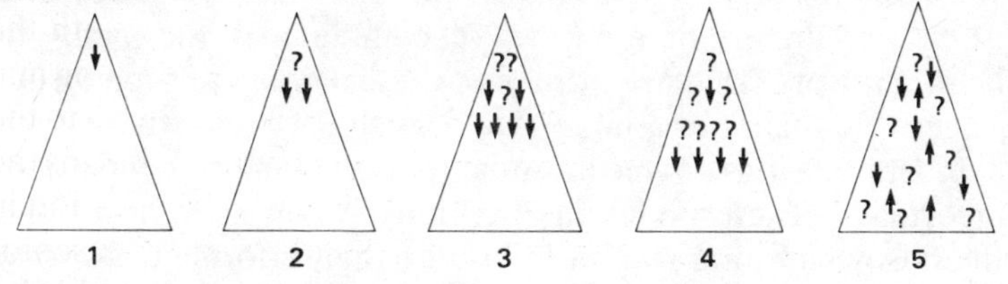

Fig 3 Top-Down organisation change

The ScotRail strategy looks more like a planned military campaign: secure your beachhead, secure your source of supply, then work on the area in between.

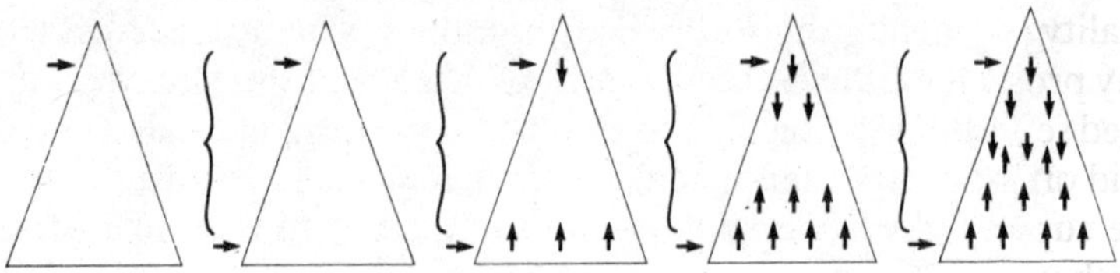

Fig 4 ScotRail's strategy for organisation change

In this strategy, the top team represent the beachhead. They were strongly committed to abolishing the bureaucracy in any way they could, and they made this known. However the second line of attack was not the middle managers so much as the junior managers, supervisors, and staff. Get these people committed to the war on bureaucracy, and you have done three things: you have abolished the bureaucracy at the coal-face, where it affects the customers; you have ensured that a generation with a lifetime's contribution to make does not have to un-learn unhelpful lessons; and you have started the pincer movement on the middle managers, who find that their bosses and their subordinates are thinking differently from them. Various activities and programmes were started in order to unfreeze the junior staff or prevent them from freezing. The increased delegation of authority helped. The Ullswater programme for junior managers and supervisors (about which more in Chapter Seven) had the objective of teaching people to challenge constraints. New selection criteria, plus the fact that ScotRail was getting a reputation as a good place to do one's management training, helped to get on board people of quite a different make-up from what had gone before. Supervisors and junior managers were involved in briefing groups, in a performance appraisal system, in organising customer care conferences, etc.

One very important move, not yet completed, is the change in the supervisory structure from one where a group of supervisors collectively managed a large group of staff to one where each member of staff knew who his supervisor was, and vice versa. It is important because under the previous system, where no one supervisor had total responsibility for the performance of one individual, it was easy for the small performance problems to go undetected or uncorrected; why should one supervisor with high standards bother to tell someone off for not wearing his hat when the next one had slacker norms? This 'floating supervisor' problem was probably responsible in large part for the poor quality of industrial relations on the railway, because the only way problems were detected were when they became so big as to need severe discipline. At an extra cost in manpower, which soon paid off in terms of less time lost dealing with disciplinary cases, the supervisory structure was revised so that each man had a 'Father in God' to whom he reported on a regular basis.

There was also deliberate, planned accelerated promotion for people who showed a capacity to manage the new style with gusto. Some of the leaps through the grades have been extraordinary, and well-deserved.

Thus, the pincer strategy. We have been rather rude about middle managers. Truth to tell, most of the middle managers responded with eagerness to the new climate – things were being done which they'd hankered after for years, and many of the best bureaucracy-busters came from the middle management ranks.

New interiors, first-class coaching stock

But what of the ones who could not take it? And there were some, indeed, who could not: the railway for far too long had become 'charitable' for too many undeserving malingerers, often at the expense of the genuine cases where special arrangements could have been made to use the individual's available skills.

In general, they were given two or three chances, and perhaps the offer of a job which would be more congenial. Then, if they could not take the new way of doing things, they had to go. Some managers have been fired, or sent to other parts of the railway (in the case of at least one transfer, the average intelligence of ScotRail and the receiving department both increased as a result). It's a policy which Peter Argent of British Airways, talking about what that organisation did in similar circumstances, called **tough love**: you help people all you can, but then they have to go. And in at least one case, the news that a manager had been fired for poor performance did wonders for staff morale.

Vivian Chadwick has on his wall the following quotation:

> 'Remember that in any household, fellowship or company that is well run, arrangements must be made that everyone in it should help and further its prosperity according to his skill or ability, and he who will not do so, unless he is there out of charity, must be expelled from the household, fellowship, or company.'
> *John Paston, 15 January 1465*

MAKE RISK-TAKING EASIER

Encouraging people to take risks is not easy in an organisation so dominated by the need for safety at all costs. Distinguishing between **safety** risk on the one hand, and **commercial** or **people** risk on the other, takes an effort in an organisation where risk has been a dirty word.

You can't encourage risk-taking without giving people the authority to take decisions and the resources to support them, so the delegation of authority downwards was a necessary part of encouraging risk-taking. Then you need a climate in which successful risk-takers are publicly praised, and unsuccessful risk-takers judged on their merits; 'We don't mind if you make mistakes, provided that they're not silly and you don't make the same mistake twice.' One small example from the Area Operations Manager on the West Highland Line: 'We've got steam on the line in the summer. I wanted to have some special souvenir tickets printed so that people would have something to remember. I was told that special tickets were not printed; that if I'd wanted special tickets I would have to go through Crewe; and that they should have been ordered in November for use in summer. So I nipped round the corner and got some printed by a local printer. I supposed I'll get chewed off for it, but by the time they've found out, I'll have made my money.' He didn't get chewed off; he was told Well Done, thou Good and Faithful Servant. And in the furnishing of the new Travel Centre at Glasgow Central a number of non-standard items were purchased locally despite protests from the Finance and Supplies Managers, who were not happy that the system had been bucked; the manager concerned took a risk, and won. Valerie Stewart remembers with delight Vivian Chadwick's gleeful recounting of the story of the junior manager at a station (which had better be anonymous) set in a local beauty spot. Coach operators had taken to using the station car park, without paying, and depriving rail customers of their facility. After repeated protests through orthodox channels, the junior manager took a high-pressure hose to the inside of one of the coaches. It worked: Vivian was obviously torn between loving the spirit of the action, and wishing that the chap had tried wheel-clamps first.

Another important factor in encouraging risk-taking is that the boss must admit it when he gets it wrong. One senior manager caused some raised eyebrows in a consultation meeting where a particular personnel practice was under discussion; he was expected by the staff to try to defend it. Instead, he admitted that it was wrong and indefensible. There is no point in posturing, and no point at all in taking risks on inadequate data, which is what you get if you don't admit mistakes.

ENCOURAGE INNOVATION

Encouraging innovation is like encouraging risk-taking: talk about it a lot, visibly reward the successful innovations; be forgiving when the intentions are right but the results don't work out.

Innovation on the railway is somewhat circumscribed by legal restrictions which prevent the kind of movement into new areas which other businesses might consider. For example, the railway has only recently been allowed to move back into road transport as a contractual addition to its services rather than a substitute for them. However, there have been some remarkably successful innovations within these limits:

Train catering, for example, was given a complete re-think. It had been intended that trolley services of light refreshments would be offered on Inter-City 125 services when the train was brought into service; later this was thought not to be possible because of problems the luggage in the aisles, etc. However, trolley services were successfully introduced on a number of ScotRail services, starting with the Edinburgh–Glasgow service. Staff acceptance was ensured by putting the service on trains where there had been no service before, i.e. the new service did not displace existing jobs. Once it had been shown to work (the Edinburgh–Glasgow service is the most profitable route on Travellers-Fare Scotland now) it was introduced on many other ScotRail lines which would not support a buffet car.

And the West Coast Main Line, from Euston, was chosen as the test-bed for a new style of on-train meals: cooked and chilled on-shore, and microwaved on the train. They allow a much wider and more attractive range of meals to be offered, such as duck a l'orange and chili con carne as well as the standard steaks and salads.

Innovation in design was encouraged, and is obvious in the way stations have been refurbished. Imaginative use of colour; lots of flowers and shops on stations; bars and lounges so attractive that they bring in people who are not rail travellers. Bars such as Tropics, Berlins, Deja Vu, and Berties are recognised as examples of excellent design surpassing many others outside the railway. The new shopping facilities in Edinburgh, and the soon-to-be-provided shopping mall in Glasgow Central are all excellent examples of the new design philosophy.

One of the most interesting technical innovations is the introduction of radio electronic token block signalling on the North Highland Line. One Signalling Centre at Dingwall closed 20 signal boxes and controls over 240 miles of track and had many side benefits. Previously communication between driver and signalman happens when the driver stops the train at a signal post telephone and phones or walks to the signal-box – an action requiring a scramble down the side of the train, and not the most pleasant of tasks in rough winter weather. This obviously causes delays to the service, and the only way that the signalman can tell the driver he wants to talk to him is by setting a signal at red and waiting for the driver to climb out of his cab. Radio signalling means that either side can initiate a conversation, with the train on the move, and gives the driver visual authority in his cab to traverse a given section of line. The actual installation is an interesting technical challenge, because of the complex nature of the task and the difficult terrain, and the need to operate to the highest standards of safety and security. Extension to the West Highland Line from Glasgow to Oban and Mallaig will be completed in 1987.

Perhaps one of the most extraordinary innovations in public relations was the decision of John Boyle, Director of Public Affairs, to publish a full-colour ScotRail Review in the September 1985 edition of *Modern Railways*. Presented like a top-notch company prospectus, it had articles, features, and photographs about all kinds of ScotRail activities: train naming ceremonies, station refurbishment, staff matters, the ScotRail Young Person of the Year, and so on. It was a bold stroke which signalled to employees and the outside world alike that ScotRail was on the move.

Busting bureaucracy is not easy. It needs constant watchfulness, and attention to detail as well as the big picture. The overall aim is to empower people to use their initiative. As we write, the Congressional Enquiry into the Space Shuttle disaster is taking place. From what one can tell so far, it is a classic example of bureaucracy gone wild. The people at the bottom and middle of the hierarchy had their suspicions that a gasket would fail under the prevailing weather conditions. They did what they could to alert top management, whose response seems to have been: 'We've committed to a programme and we're going to stick to it.' One of the warnings even came from an accountant, who noticed a rise in component failures associated with a drop in temperatures; he was ignored because, being an accountant, he couldn't possibly have anything useful to say about engineering matters. Stick to the plan; ignore unwelcome information; take away people's motivation and authority – and in this case, their lives. That's bureaucracy at its most obviously destructive, but how many people live their working lives feeling that any possible achievement they might have in mind will be negated by the bureaucrats, the rules, the system which has been around so long that it cannot be changed?

ScotRail has in its 1986 Operating Plan a different statement: that authority is what you take, not what somebody gives you. The evidence is that when people are empowered to take authority, they outstrip what had been thought possible. Perhaps we can finish this chapter by quoting Jimmy Allan, Area Manager at Edinburgh Waverley Station:

> 'I always felt that Mr. Green was an excellent leader and he certainly led a first-class team. The General Manager cut across all the boundaries of departmental influence and people had to be big to accept the situation.
>
> 'The Area Managers' liberation was an important by-product of busting the bureaucracy. It was not what was said, but rather what was not said, allied to a complete turn around in management style by the Regional Operating Manager that made the changes possible. Area Managers and HQ Staff of all departments spoke freely and confidently: this was new.
>
> 'I am still not sure that those who didn't know the old fully appreciate the new.'

7 · Personnel and Training Policies

Salaries wages, and related costs account for over 60 per cent of the British Railways Board's total expenditure – approximately £3,096 million. Probably 75 per cent or more of the customer's image of the railway is determined by the kind of treatment he gets from the staff. Equipment failures are understandable, though very annoying if one is caught in them; what the customer does not understand is the failure of railway personnel to offer information. Comfortable trains get taken for granted after a while, but a member of staff who looks as if he's pleased to see you stays in the mind for a long time. Lots of customers would rather make enquiries in person than trust to their reading of the timetable: how much nicer if the person they deal with looks efficient and seems to want your business. Yet the amount of money spent on getting the right staff in the right jobs, with the right training, is ridiculously small; a capital-intensive industry will spend between 8 per cent and 15 per cent on preventive maintenance on its equipment, and a good sum on investment appraisal, but labour-intensive industries do not have the same sense of urgency about doing preventive maintenance on the payroll budget.

VOCATIONAL TRAINING

The history of personnel and training policies on the railway is typical of many organisations which derive their history from military and/or government example. Most training was vocational in the strictest sense, i.e. training in how to operate the equipment or procedures one was charged with looking after. This training was often not related to the needs of the individual: thus, a driving course might well teach the recipient to drive classes of locomotive he would never encounter, or had only a remote chance of encountering long after the lessons learned in the training had disappeared into oblivion. And the person's training needs were determined not by analysis of the gap between his present skills and those required to do the new job, but by agreement with the trade unions, who would negotiate a fixed length of time to train irrespective of the person's rate of progress or previous knowledge.

Aspects of the vocational training are very good indeed, and one has only to look at the railway's safety record to see this. But other training needs which would be recognised by many other organisations went largely unmet: management training, for example, consisted of long courses which served to weld people together as a team but gave them little insight into how other industries managed themselves. People who would have profited from a visit to Marks & Spencer, or ICI, or some of their customers' factories, went on tours to see railways in other countries. Getting a short course on, say, report-writing or public speaking was very difficult. There was, and in many cases still is, little link between the need for particular types of training and its supply. People could have been listed for a course for years before being offered it. The links between the supply of new equipment and the training of people to use it are often imperfect: for example, the APTIS system of computerised ticket sales has suffered considerable delays, but this information was not communicated to the training staff in time for them to redeploy the resources they had set aside to train booking office staff in its use. And many groups of people who really needed training in, say, man-management found it difficult to get: supervisors, for example, for whom the man-management part of the job is often the most difficult, are offered a NEBSS course (NEBSS = National Educational Board for Supervisory Studies) but this is of limited relevance and may not become available until several years after promotion. Whereas the military sensibly puts its best people into the training function and gives them the appropriate status, railway instructors often lost out in terms of opportunities for overtime, etc., and it is not seen automatically as a good career move to have some time as an instructor. In many cases, too, the facilities and equipment for training were abysmally poor: the ScotRail training centre used to be at Polmadie, in an old bomb-proof storehouse, without facilities for people who may have come to a training course after a full shift even to get themselves a hot meal. Assigning staff to training courses is the task of the roster clerk, which means that staff may be pulled out of training at short notice in order to attend to operational duties (not a bad thing: the poor customer wouldn't take well to an announcement that his train was cancelled due to staff training); more disturbingly, it is by no means uncommon for them to roster someone to the second day of a course before he's had the first.

And, of course, staff training was always one of the first things to be cut when more money had to be found out of the budget to meet a down-turn in revenue. This practice is by no means confined to the railway, of course; plenty of people have commented that some at least of Britain's industrial decline can be attributed to the fact that in economic crisis our industries cut down on training while other countries increase theirs.

RECRUITMENT

For an organisation which appoints nearly all its managers from within, the recruitment practices were similarly messy and wasteful. The recruitment of wages grade staff suffered because of the poor starting wage, which makes it difficult to attract good school-leavers in certain parts of the country. Even when enough people could be encouraged to apply, they would be interviewed in an unsystematic way, often by an administration clerk who had little or no experience of the jobs for which he was interviewing. One exercise at King's Cross attracted over 80 recruits – before the present levels of unemployment – of whom after six months only one person was still with the railway. Sloppy recruitment practices were made worse in many cases by poor induction and initial experience. For example, if you joined as a booking clerk your first experience would probably be in the telephone enquiry bureau. Answering telephone queries about the railway service is in fact a more skilled and in some ways more demanding task than – say – answering questions face-to-face in a fairly quiet booking office. You would do it with minimum training in railway geography and time-tabling. Two examples will suffice, both from Valerie Stewart's experience: one happened when she sat in on a TEB training course in Glasgow and found that the instructor was advising the class to tell their customers to allow two hours to travel from King's Cross or Euston to Heathrow Airport. It transpired in later discussions that none of them had ever been to London and made cross-London connections of any kind. The second example is of the time when she found herself as rearguard in a queue of two in Reading Information Office. The queue was not moving. Listening hard, she learned that the lady in front of her wanted to travel to Effingham Junction, and the clerk was looking it up under the letter F. In general, the recruitment practices can be criticised as demoralised and unscientific, and the induction as narrow and unsupportive.

If recruitment of staff can be so criticised, what about the recruitment of management trainees? In the mainly technical areas this was not bad: the technical content of the job is obvious and there is a direct link between quality of degree subject and likely success in the technical job. But the recruitment practices in the non-technical grades were less than satisfactory in a number of ways: first, it was difficult to transfer from being a technical trainee to being a personnel or marketing trainee, for example. So two career streams were effectively created, and the non-technical grades tended to get more rapid promotion. Second, there was a constant resentment by the staff of these younger people who came in, in their early 20's, at grades which the staff had struggled for years to attain. Most supervisors have stories of the amount of support they have had to offer to someone who was nominally their superior: 'Don't you think we should turn the current off before we go down on the line, Sir?' In a way, it is like the advice an experienced nurse will give to a rookie doctor, but it is not helped by the fact that staff who wish to try for the management training scheme had until recently a very early cut-off age (28) before their chances disappeared. And, of course, there was the stated or unconscious bias against women, which is now being remedied.

INDUSTRIAL RELATIONS

Industrial relations were often adversarial, concerned with controlling and outwitting the staff rather than getting the best out of them. A symptom of the systemisation crisis is the delegation of all or nearly all staff contact to the trade unions. This was certainly the case on the railway, a situation connived at by management and unions together. In many ways, it was in neither party's interest for the managers to start talking directly to the staff. In an industry where three unions were more or less at war with each other – ASLEF, traditionally the most powerful union, experienced a drop in membership and a de-skilling of the work their members do, while the NUR's relative power base increased – it was difficult for the management to get whole-hearted and unanimous union agreement. There were a number of bruising confrontations, including a series of one-day strikes in 1982 over the issue of flexible rostering which caused a permanent drop in business and induced a number of important freight customers to move to road transport or at least go in for dual-sourcing. Some of the confrontations were made worse by poor negotiating practice, where the negotiators were more concerned to get an acceptable form of words than to achieve a resolution that would have success on implementation. Many of the other failures in personnel policy could be attributed to over-centralisation and a strong tendency to look inwards. The managerial performance appraisal system is one such example. Performance appraisal should be a means for enabling a structured and thorough discussion to take place between boss and subordinate. In many organisations other itmes were added to this agenda: the collection of information about training needs, career aspirations, promotion potential, and so on. Some organisations went on to add Management by Objectives, and some to link the performance rating to pay. The effect of adding all these external issues to the discussion is often (not always) disabling, and many organisations have simplified their appraisal

Old barriers Glasgow Central

system to get back to a straightforward discussion between boss and subordinate.

The railway appraisal system committed just about every systematic fault available to it. The worst was the linking of the appraisal rating directly to pay. This turns the discussion from a forward look at the future to a raking over the coals of the past as both parties seek to justify their opinion. It makes it difficult to have a discussion about training needs, for who is going to freely talk about his strengths and waknesses when he knows it will cost him money for every weakness he admits. As if that were not bad enough, the central personnel function issued an edict that managers had to assign their appraisal ratings according to the normal distribution. This is just not possible to achieve without doing irrepairable damage to the original purposes of the system. In an established team of experienced people the ratings will naturally skew towards the top end of the scale; in a team of inexperienced people they will skew towards the bottom. The Chief Civil Engineer of one Region put it succinctly: 'I am answerable in a coroner's court if there is a fatal accident within my jurisdiction. And I am supposed to stand up in front of the coroner and say that according to the latest wisdom from the Personnel Department I am supposed to have half my team of below average standards.'

PERSONNEL

With this degree of ineptitude it might be thought that the Personnel Department would lack power. Unfortunately this was not so. In some key areas the power they held was too great. For example, they were often committed to enforcing the rule that the most senior applicant rather than the most suitable should be appointed to a post long after line managers were trying to abandon this practice. Many trivial issues which a line manager could have settled by face-to-face discussion with the person concerned were instead delegated to the Personnel function, acting alone or in negotiation with the trade unions; there they suffered the same fate as the minor works which were delegated to the engineering functions – they became low priority in combination with all the other claims on Personnel time, and they became issues which could be conceded in negotiations on larger matters.

The remoteness is perhaps best illustrated by a story from

Vivian Chadwick's experience when at Bradford. In those times staff did not get sick pay. He therefore went directly to the staff and offered to pay people who were sick, provided that his total wage bill did not increase as a result. In effect, he was asking other staff to double up for their absent colleagues; he was also introducing a much stronger control over malingering than could ever have been implemented by authority, because the staff would exert their own control over any mates thought to be skiving. The response from the Personnel Department (when they found out) was not one of delight, or seeing what could be learned for the rest of the railway; it was: 'You can't do that,' even though there was nothing in the rules that said he couldn't. The experiment managed to survive for six months.

We have painted a fairly black picture. It is getting better on the whole of the railway. An injection of new blood has helped: the Management Studies Centre at Watford is now headed by Roger Stuart, who has had experience in a variety of outside industries and has re-vamped considerably the range of courses on offer. Many of the new people coming into the personnel function are professionally trained and business-aware, and it shows in the way there are trying to turn the Personnel Department into an enabling function.

On ScotRail there were many innovations in personnel practice, of which we shall single out just a few. They were spearheaded by a very capable Regional Personnel Manager – Peter Woods – and a top management team committed to caring for the staff and creating a climate in which they could all perform at their peak. (Valerie Stewart will embarrass her co-author when she says that she has never seen a line manager so committed to people: when she runs courses for him, she gets a briefing about each person who is attending – and this is about junior staff, from someone who had at the time 8,000 people on his payroll. And when the tutor on an Ullswater supervisors' course had to drop out through last-minute illness, Viv immediately gave up his day off to help on the course. He can stay embarrassed; it needs saying, and I'm writing this bit.)

Of the many innovations, we shall look at six: training, communications strategy, staff accommodation, equal opportunities, enhancement of management authority and experience, and supervisor development.

TRAINING

Training was given a new and higher priority. For managers, Strathclyde Business School was engaged to provide one-week management skills courses, which have been well received, and there have been courses in self-development and personnel management at Stirling University.

The one-week residential course in Basic Management Skills was another of the offspring spawned by the Employee Development Policy. Previously all management training at this level had been carried out centrally at 'The Grove', British Railways Board's Management Training Centre at Watford. The Watford courses themselves were, and still are, highly relevant in content and professional in presentation; but with a staff of mere human beings The Grove found it impossible to meet consistently the training needs of all five Regions on BR as well as those of Headquarters and Business staff, particularly with the insistent 'bottom-line' mentality which was evolving at this time and creating an increasing demand on The Grove to provide managers with the skills required to respond appropriately.

Within ScotRail it was quickly realised that Regional training for ScotRail managers was the only way to ensure the full satisfaction of training needs. In addition, the 'branding' of the Region had caught on strongly and a definite Scottish dimension was emerging. With a Regional training strategy this could be captured and developed to best advantage.

In developing a new Regional stategy for training and development, contact was made with many professional and academic authorities outside BR in order to capitalise on the expertise available. The Strathclyde Business School was of course one of these and in July 1985 it hosted a two-week pilot course on Management Skills Development. From this pilot the most relevant content and appropriate style of presentation were identified, leading to the development of the current one-week programme.

The Effective Management Skills course aims to build managerial knowledge at junior management level and develop skills and potential within the railway industry. Participants examine basic principles in the key areas of management, identify their own managerial style, consider the opportunities and constraints in applying their skills, and formulate action plans to improve their performance and develop further as effective managers.

On three out of the four evening sessions senior managers attended from ScotRail (including the General Manager or Deputy General Manager) on a voluntary basis as guest speakers, sharing their own experiences and views on effective management and leading lively and informal discussion sessions with participants. These sessions are invaluable in helping participants to integrate their new learning with the realities of implementing a professional management style on a day-to-day basis. They also provide a unique opportunity for questioning senior managers about short, medium, and long-term strategies for the future of the railway.

The course itself is residential, partly through necessity because of the late finishing times, but mainly in order to allow the productive exchange of ideas and opinions which inevitably form much of the bar conversations following each day's final session. Such conversations are also a very useful source of feedback in addition to the 'official version' provided on end-of-course evaluation forms. What follows is a selection of typical comments from both the above sources:

> 'Gave me the perspective and words to identify situations that either I knew were happening or had previously experienced but had not fully appreciated. It has also introduced new ways of tackling problems that I just didn't have time to sit down and work out before.'
>
> 'I never realised just how much the Scottish Region were doing, especially compared with other Regions. It makes you proud, doesn't it?'
>
> 'It is a great morale booster that ScotRail has identified the training needs of junior management staff and is prepared to spend money on satisfying them.'
>
> 'I think it was indicative of the group's keenness that on the one free evening all the group returned to the classroom to view and review one another's performance on the video workshops.'
>
> 'It brought home to me that management is about people; it's not just budgets, equipment, and administration. I began to think and to re-assess my views in a more positive manner.'
>
> 'The visiting BR speakers were a most useful addition to the course. They were surprisingly informal and it was very helpful to get their views on how we should be acting as professional managers. It also helped us to see exactly where ScotRail was going – looking forward instead of looking back.'

Staff training was revolutionised first by dynamiting the old school at Polmadie and building a completely new school at Rutherglen. The Rutherglen school has taken on new tasks; has got the best possible equipment; and some very good staff. Customer Care training gets 3 days – other Regions try to do it in a day or less. The standard of the Customer Care training, which was designed by George Lafferty with extraordinary creativity and flair, is so high that many organisations in Scotland and outside have asked to borrow it. Still to be achieved is a re-negotiation of some of the old ways of designing and assessing training; many of the courses could be shortened and made better if people were assessed on what they needed to know and the progress they were making, rather than being tied by national agreements to a fixed curriculum and a given length of time.

COMMUNICATIONS STRATEGY

Communications strategy means two things: making sure that people know what's going on, and making sure that they get it through their own manager. A good communications strategy pre-empts the rumour network, and pre-empts the trade unions if they have a record of selective communication. A good communications strategy has another necessary feature: it is **two-way**. In a big organisation in particular it is easy for managers to become out of touch with the work-force; communication should involve listening as much as telling.

Some aspects of the communications strategy are routine. There is now a high-quality newsletter published for ScotRail staff only; it began shortly after Chris Green was appointed General Manager, and served amongst other things to do the necessary establishing of him and the rest of the team as new and trustworthy blood. It tells the bad news as well as the good news, not hesitating to draw attention to failures as well as successes. It was used to tell the remoter parts of ScotRail what was happening by way of refurbishment of the network, and to assure them that their time would come soon. It was used to promote news of competitions and innovations – for example the ScotRail Young Person of the Year award, started in 1985 and continuing as a way of promoting excellence and community service.

Another routine but important part of the strategy is the Briefing Group. In these, in which everybody is supposed to be involved, information cascades from the top down by way of meetings at which managers at all levels meet with their staff to talk about what's going on. There may be particular issues on the agenda, or it may be just an open discussion. The briefing groups were preceded by training for managers in how to run them – perhaps a small point, but another earnest of ScotRail's commitment to training. Many attempts in other organisations to introduce briefing groups fail because managers are not properly trained to conduct them, or do not see how important it is that they respond quickly to the staff's queries.

One important function which these routine channels service is the giving of praise. Managers can and do use them as a way of telling their staff that they are proud of them for a job well done. In an industry which gets far more kicks than thank-you's, praise is a commodity in short supply. It's easy to forget to give it; one of the warmest-hearted Area Managers, Matt MacAteer of North Clyde, said in a meeting that he had not had a single word of complaint about his staff all year. 'Have you told them that, Matt?' someone asked. He hadn't, but he did.

Other communications efforts are non-routine. In the guards' dispute of 1985 there was a special 'hot-line' where people could phone and talk about their concerns. The important thing here is that there was a real person on the other end of the phone, not a recorded message telling them that they were sheep for obeying the orders of their unions. Over ScotRail as a whole the hot-line received 27 phone calls in the period before the strike; it served not merely as a way of keeping a channel actively open to the staff, but because line managers were drawn into the 'answering service' it brought home to them yet again that industrial relations are a line responsibility, not something you leave to the Personnel Department to worry about.

Efforts to persuade the staff that you want to train them better and communicate with them directly can earn a cynical response if the other indicators of management attitude are not right. Staff accommodation has been rebuilt in every case of station refurbishment, with better facilities for meals, toilets, and making use of the enforced leisure that is present even in the most efficient train diagram. In addition all the larger Train Crew depots have had new accommodation constructed, generally on the stations themselves rather than on the sites of the old steam depots as was traditional. All but the smallest depots will be in a similar accommodation by 1987/88. And, as we have already said, the philosophy on uniforms, equipment, etc., has changed so that people are looking for excellence rather than the cheapest possible.

EQUAL OPPORTUNITIES

Equal Opportunities for women have become a matter of concern and action. It is easy to get bogged down in words here, or to push the problem onto someone else. (Valerie Stewart doesn't much care for organised groups of women lamenting their problems, but went along when invited to a Women in British Rail conference at the British Railways Board. We did the traditional thing of breaking into small groups to identify the problem; our small group contained lots of well-dressed ladies in marketing and personnel, two operating trainees, and an Indian lady who was a clerk at Liverpool Street Travel Centre and thought she had been badly done by. The group lamented that male attitudes were the problem and would have to change, etc., etc. After making a few phone calls at the beginning of lunch I came back to find all the white women sitting gossiping over their chicken legs and the Indian lady eating alone and excluded. Motes, beams, etc.)

There is an Equal Opportunities group on ScotRail. So far, we have decided to do everything we can to promote ScotRail as an equal opportunity employer, by contact with careers services, advertising on stations, contact with Parent–Teacher associations, etc. A largely all-male organisation which is about to welcome more women needs changes in facilities like loos, changing rooms, etc. One important decision made after talking to some women in roles previously performed by men is that in future a woman will not be appointed to a post where she is the only woman in her grade – not for reasons of physical safety, but because men tend to judge all women by the faults and failings of the ones they see, and the singleton women felt that they were making a case not only for themselves but for all women.

These strategies will cope to some extent with the problem of getting equal opportunity of entry to the railway. What about the people presently employed? How are more women to be attracted to middle management jobs? This is one of the more difficult problems to solve, but there is always a good resource available untapped – most secretaries of any seniority are good managers. They have to be. So there is to be a programme, open to anybody but publicised particularly to women, where people can come for a day and get a taste of the management job to see if they feel they have any management potential.

However equal opportunities is as much about equal opportunities for **all** staff with no artificial distinctions, such as those which exist between salaried and wages grade staff. The thrust to get more women into management is probably easier than that to break down the years of traditional division between those who collect their pay weekly and those who get it monthly.

And why is this being done? Not out of trendiness. In the words of Chris Green, who chaired the group when he was General Manager and passed the chairmanship onto the new General Manager: 'I'm doing this because I'm tired of not having access to the skills and abilities of half the work-force.'

He said this, incidentally, chairing the group on the morning when the results of the guards' strike ballot were due to be announced. What better example could there be of good management in action: that the General Manager should trust his team to handle the current crisis while he gets on with the job of making tomorrow better?

Driver operating Radio Electronic Token Block on Kyle of Lochalsh Line

ENHANCEMENT OF MANAGEMENT AUTHORITY AND EXPERIENCE

Enhancement of management authority and experience is a permanent item on the agenda. We have already mentioned their increased authority to spend investment money and make operating decisions. On the personnel side, too, authority had been increased. They are under an obligation to pay most attention to suitability rather than the traditional seniority methods when promoting someone. Many of them have organised their own local training courses for staff. Bob Heasman, the Area Manager for Tayside, organises a team-building event once a year for the group of managers who report to him. Most of the managers have some sort of team-building activity built onto their objectives: one had an objective to get the whole of his team up Ben Nevis before the year end. There's nothing about Ben Nevis that has to do with running the railway, but getting the whole team up it says a lot about team-work and mutual trust.

One of the most responsible jobs on the railway, even if the skills have changed somewhat, is that of driver. The drivers used to complain that management did not understand their case because managers had never been drivers. So all the Area Managers were put on a driving course (much to the horror of ASLEF); and sure enough, the world does look different from the driver's cab.

SUPERVISORY DEVELOPMENT

One of the most important parts of the personnel and training strategy has been the concentration on **supervisory development**. Much of the day-to-day running of the railway is in the hands of supervisors, and yet as in most industries theirs is one of the least well-defined and well-rewarded jobs. Many supervisors on ScotRail now have authority to conduct the first stage of the disciplinary procedure; national discussions to develop this approach nationally will soon take place. There have been two other important changes: a pilot performance appraisal system for supervisors to use with their staff, and the Ullswater courses for supervisors and junior managers.

Introducing a simple appraisal system for supervisors to use with their staff creates and enforces the opportunity for dialogue between the two. It is easy, given the geographical separation between stations, for supervisors in the rural parts of ScotRail not to see their staff except on special visits. The agenda for these visits is usually determined by whatever is urgent and causing problems. It is easy to neglect discussion of the future in favour of current problem-solving. It is easy for both parties to have widely differing views about what kind of performance is expected. So, the appraisal system – much simpler than the Board system, definitely not tied to pay, and derived from discussion with supervisors themselves – will help them achieve joint standard-setting and working towards improving the service; and it is yet another sign, for those who are looking for one, that the supervisors can be trusted to do a good job.

THE ULLSWATER EXPERIENCE

Mention of **trust** takes us to the final example of personnel policy in action – the Ullswater courses for senior supervisors and junior managers. This is a one-week course, held at Ullswater in the Lake District, designed partly for personal development and partly for organisation development.

The courses had their beginning in a conversation between Vivian Chadwick and Valerie Stewart. At our very first meeting we discovered that we shared a common passion for getting better training for managers and supervisors who had not come though the formal management training system – those people who had left school early, not gone to University, and by their late 20's or early 30's were holding down posts of huge responsibility with very little training or acknowledgement of their contribution. We dropped whatever we were supposed to be talking about in favour of plotting something good for these people.

The Ullswater courses are held in the outdoors, but they do not teach outdoor skills. The outdoors is used for three reasons: first, that people cannot put on their conference eyes and pretend they're there – they have to participate or they are seen not to. Second, the consequences of their actions are very real: you can talk all you like in a classroom about planning, organising, and controlling, but you learn how good you are when you're at the top of the mountain and the sandwiches are at the bottom. Third, the memory for what goes on is technicolour: whereas one might remember 10 per cent of what happens on an ordinary course, one might retain 30 or 40 per cent of what happens in the outdoors.

The course has an agenda, which different groups tackle at different speeds. They begin by looking at 'myself as a manager' – do I do what I say I do, and if not, why not? Then they go on to look at 'myself as a person' – what are my particular strengths, and how can I use the different strengths of other people around me? Finally they look at 'myself in the organisation' – what have I learned on this course that I can take back with me to contribute to the changing world of ScotRail.

In the course of the week, their focus of attention shifts radically from **procedures** to **people**. In the beginning, asked what a good manager does, their answers contain lots of words like planning, organising, setting objectives, and so on. Later in the week they are starting to examine and experience the real issues involved in managing change – issues to do with trust, paying attention to individual needs and motivation, and – crucially – busting the bureaucracy. You cannot ask people to do new things unless they trust you, and ScotRail is asking people to do new things every day. When you are operating in the 'unknown solutions to unknown problems' box, policies and procedures are very little use; you have to have faith in one another's abilities as well. And if you have never abseiled before, and you are being let over the edge of a cliff by someone else who has never abseiled before, then it's of limited help to know that the safety instructors have checked that all the rules have been followed. Actually to go over the edge requires trust, and the memory of the necessity of that trust is something that carries on back to the work-place.

About 30 per cent of the time on the Ullswater courses is spent in the classroom, reviewing what has happened. Some of the participants have said, some time later, that these are the sessions they remember the best. The classroom sessions include psychological testing and individual feedback (using the test described in Chapter Nine on team-building), and a day in which the Regional Operations Manager or other Functional Manager reviews their experience with them. That this is a necessary part of the course is indicated by the experience of another Region, who tried to do the same thing without the top management involvement, and failed.

So far, over 200 people have been through the course. In keeping with our original vision, we began by forbidding entry to people who had come in through the graduate entrant scheme, but nobody worries that this rule has been relaxed. Many of them find it difficult to say what it has done for them, because it is such a personal experience; but few deny that it has been productive of new insights and skills which they can take back and use. The aim is to have a critical mass of young managers who have all been through the Ullswater experience and can use this to rely on one another.

We asked Peter Farrell, one of the participants, to write about his experience in Ullswater. Here is what he said:

> 'The Ullswater Management Development Course could best be described as an 'experience'. It involves all the senses in learning about oneself and one's relative position in life and work.
>
> 'It is interesting to note that from the moment a candidate for Ullswater is advised of the pending event he or she immediately switches on – apprehension and fear of the unknown usually wrestle with a feeling of adventure and a willingness to do well for one's own sake.
>
> 'The course is designed to warm participants to one another fairly quickly and begins by encouraging them as a group to express their hopes, fears, and expectations, which are aired with an honesty that helps to break down barriers. However, it is not until the first simple and practical exercise that the group begins to find its identity; this is precipitated by the physical touching, and almost immediate willingness of each to contribute towards the group task; and by a shared humour and finally a shared failure of success which draws them together. It is them that the real learning begins to take place.
>
> 'The exercises all involve very definite tasks but the tasks themselves only present something to aim at and in the journey towards achieving these tasks the necessary interaction within the group provides the real learning. The problems presented are not those experienced in the work-place but the same decision-making processes are involved and all the external pressures of working with and in a team are there to be coped with.
>
> 'The exercises become more and more arduous and with in-depth reviews after each the lessons are learned and built upon. Management principles begin to be recognised as necessary to the success of the exercise and are highlighted and reiterated through the week – the need for organisation and planning, leadership, teamwork, good communications, thought for the individual, etc.
>
> 'A particular highlight of the course is the Myers–Briggs Type Indicator test which is offered to the participants early on in the course; it is interesting to stand back and see how the results affect them individually.

'Before the results are made known an explanation of the psychological types is given and as the explanation unfolds each anticipates his or her type. For the most parts the results confirm the expectations but there are always some who do not quite agree with the profile given them and this usually generates much discussion which continues throughout the week and carries on into the mandatory pub visits in the evenings – I suspect that by the end of the week there is greater willingness to accept the results particularly when it is made clear that each type contains commendable strengths as well as weaknesses.

'The course becomes all-consuming as each lesson is taken and savoured and carried on to the next exercise where the learning is further consolidated. At no time are the participants allowed the luxury of becoming complacent as the exercises take on new twists and which require imagination and initiative to resolve. The final exercise on the course demands much from the group and is seen as the climax of all the learning. It provides an opportunity to put all those lessons learned into practice and by virtue of the physical hurdles to be cleared in this particular exercise a great sense of personal achievement is experienced.'

As a tutor on the Ullswater courses, Valerie Stewart has some precious memories of moments of great insight:

The time when a group broke the rules because they thought no-one was looking, and then realised as they reviewed themselves that they had missed a big learning opportunity.

The time when one of the participants managed his team in a really autocratic fashion and had a strike on his hands, and the skill with which the strike committee later swallowed their feelings to bring him back into the group and help him learn the real consequences of that particular management style.

The division of one group, when presented with the briefing and resources for a long task, into those who made the decisions and those who made the sandwiches.

The participant who had had rheumatic fever as a child and didn't feel able to do anything with his arms, such as abseiling; and the other participant who saw his fears and asked him to be the safety man as **he** abseiled; and the transformation this made to the first man's view of himself as an outsider and a weakling.

The group in which no natural leader came forward and nobody took responsibility for planning the task; how they ran out of time on their abseiling task and had to return disconsolate and angry, and what a hard lesson it was for them that outdoor training is not about acquiring outdoor skills but about

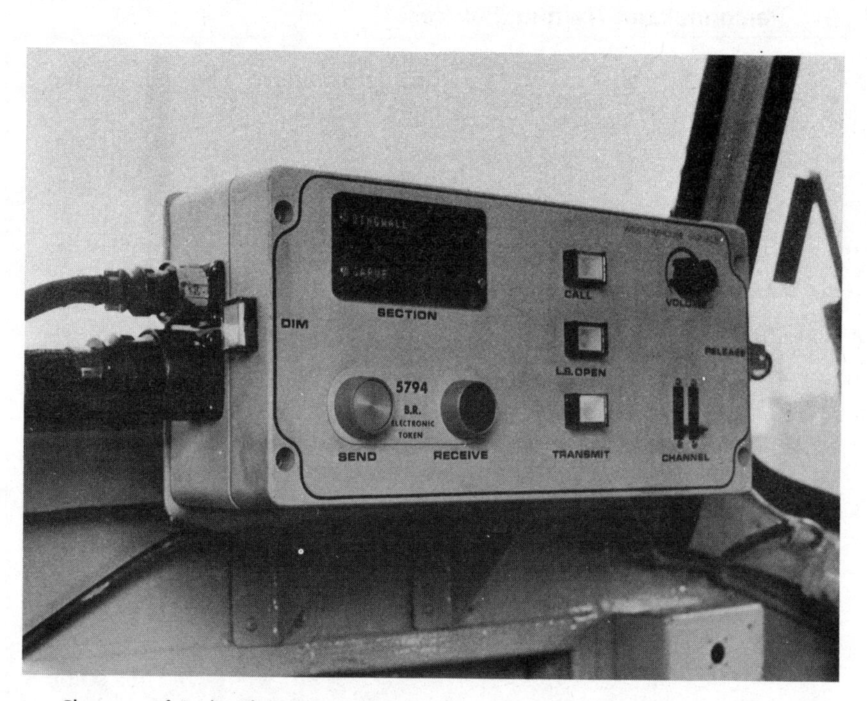

Close up of Radio Electronic Token Block instrument in cab of locomotive – Dingwall–Garve section

performing management tasks in situations where the consequences of your actions are very real and visible.

The 15-minute shared silence with which we start the day, and the feeling of people really learning to use it as the week goes on.

The Ullswater courses are one of the best things ScotRail has done to develop in future management skills; many thanks to Steve Howe, the Principal of Ullswater Outward Bound, and Pete Bramwell, the Senior Instructor, and their colleagues who sustain the programme.

Personnel and training policies are difficult things to get excited about. So we have to go back to our original point: that ScotRail is a labour-intensive industry; that it is a service industry in which people are the product; and that all the superb equipment in the world will not compensate for staff who are puzzled or grumpy or badly motivated. Superb staff cannot hold the line against bad equipment for ever: but we must finish with the story of the guard on an Inter-City 125 in the hot summer of 1983. The performance of the GEC (Paxman) engines was not up to the heat. Locomotive availability was appalling. On a long section the train broke down with engine failure. The guard came on to the intercom: 'Ladies and Gentlemen,' he said, 'I have some bad news and some good news. The bad news is that both engines have failed and it will be about an hour and a half before someone comes to rescue us. The good news is: think how much worse it would have been if we were flying.' From 400 enemies he now had 400 friends on the train.

We need more people as skilled as that. People skilled to use their initiative in difficult situations, because whatever we know about the future, we know it is not going to get any easier. That's what personnel and training policies are about.

8 · Disasters

Some of the most testing times for an organisation come when disaster strikes. The railway reactions to accidents are well-practised, even though it remains far and away the most safe form of public transport available. An accident, or another disaster, is also an opportunity for people to learn; not merely technical improvements, but matters of railway management as well.

Where natural disasters and accidents are concerned, two points are worth making. First, that all incidents involving fatal accidents to the public, and many major accidents, have to be investigated by a special team drawn originally from the Royal Engineers (a legacy of Victorian times) and the majority of the changes they recommend are implemented. Consider for a moment what the effect on car drivers would be if every fatal car accident had to be so investigated and every driver and manufacturer abide by the recommendation. By this stage in the railway's development, there are very few accidents ascribable to technical faults; most of the accidents are due to human error or vandalism, and these can be minimised but never eliminated completely.

INVESTIGATION OF DISASTERS

The second point concerns the way accidents are investigated. There is a strong tradition of honesty and full disclosure. This is perhaps not apparent except when contrasted with – say – the investigation of accidents on oil rigs. Some of the oil companies with off-shore operations have come to the railway for advice, because when they have accidents there is confusion of objectives between their own technical people, who are concerned to find out objectively what went wrong, and the police, who are concerned to establish blame or alleged criminality.

We shall look at three disasters which happened to ScotRail, not in order to give a full account of the accident but in order to see what management lessons were learned from them. The three include on civil engineering disaster – the Burnmouth Slip;

one industrial relations disaster – the 1985 guards' dispute; and one appalling accident – the Polmont crash in which 13 people were killed.

THE BURNMOUTH SLIP

On 8th May 1983, when Jim Cornell (then the Chief Civil Engineer and now the General Manager of ScotRail) had been CCE for just eight days, the land at Burnmouth slipped feet into the sea. Burnmouth is on the East Coast main line, where you get those spectacular views south of Edinburgh and north of Berwick-upon-Tweed. Here the East Coast Main Line is perched some 60 metres above the sea and the slippage of some 5,000 tonnes of material down the slope below the railway seriously threatened the stability of the Main Line. The railway line had slipped before: John Thomas's book on the North British Railway notes that in 1845 it had descended into the 'German Sea' and the grandfather of one of the gangers who worked on the 1983 slip could remember it. Needless to say, he was quizzed thoroughly about his memories.

The timing of the slip could not have been worse; following after the Penmansheil tunnel collapse, and not long after the publication of the Serpell report, on 20th January, which said that there should be no railway north of Newcastle. So, it was necessary to get it fixed, and fixed quickly; and to keep the trains running at the same time.

There was not enough time to do a massive detailed soil survey before starting the job, despite the very complicated geology which included a reverse thrust fault which Jim Cornell later described as 'adding to the interest.' Traffic was halted on the Up Line, but allowed to continue at reduced speed on the Down Line. They surveyed as they repaired; Messrs. Cornell and Chadwick were in adjacent rooms at the North British Hotel at the time, both having transferred north recently, and they each recall being woken at frequent intervals as the CCE received the reports on progress.

While drilling was carried out to asertain the nature of the underlying rock, a 2.5 metre re-alignment scheme was carried out and on 15th May both lines were re-opened to traffic at 10 mph (16 kph). As the slip worsened, two further slues, each involving earthworks and amounting in total to a 7 metre dog-leg in the track, were made to retain a safe track. The underlying rock was discovered to be too chattered to allow a bored piling solution and a major sluing scheme (of 25 metres over about 1 kilometre) involving significant earthworks was proposed and agreed.

While trains continued to run normally over the slued track, a level crossing was constructed to allow dump trucks to transfer and tip the excavated material from the landward to the seaward side of the line. This crossing carried 100 trains and 800 30-ton dumpers per day for some six weeks.

250,000 cubic metres (about half a tonne) of soil and rock were dug, ripped, and blasted to form the new cutting. Drainage and fencing works and even a new road to a farm had to be constructed, but the final track slues onto a prepared formation took place on the weekends of 17/18 and 24/25 September and the East Coast Main Line was re-opened to a speed of 90 mph (144 kph) on 30th September.

Only one week of single line working and four additional 8-hour possessions were required for all this work, which was carried out by the Civil Engineers and their contractors at a cost of £1,625,000.

The experience pulled all sorts of talent out of the engineering function – talent that nobody had realised was there. And it produced a great deal of interfunctional co-operation; not merely in the marshalling of resources to meet the disaster, but in the re-routing of trains and the conveying of information to the customers. Staff at Carstairs had to cope with a considerable increase in traffic, dealing with an HST shuttle service from Edinburgh which fed into the West Coast Main Line route, and a through HST service to London Kings Cross. Bob Rogers, one of the supervisors concerned, recollects the unusual sight of an HST to Kings Cross on one platform and a West Coast Electric Service on the other. A buffet service was provided in what is now the night ticket hall. Carstairs during this period had also to deal with re-routed freight services and all in all were faced with a mammoth increase in traffic; but in the finest traditions of the railway service the staff rose to the challenge and look back on this episode with some considerable pride in a job well done. Bob and his colleagues all freely admit that this was an enjoyable though taxing time in their railway experience.

THE 1985 GUARDS' DISPUTE

Some trains are capable of being operated without guards. These are trains working suburban routes, with sliding doors that can be operated by the driver, where the operating requirements for having a guard on the train have dwindled to zero. The role of the guard on freight trains has also diminished.

The proposal was put forward nationally to take the guards out of the operating role and give them more duties involving revenue protection and customer care. On ScotRail the proposed action was slightly different from the national one: under the Strathclyde Manning Agreement trains would be designed to run without guards; guards would be asked to do customer care and revenue protection duties, and the expectation would be that of having a guard on the train; the major difference being that if for any reason the guard could not be there, the train would leave anyway.

The national dispute overtook any disagreements about the Strathclyde Manning Agreement, and in the beginning the unions undoubtedly had the communications advantage. They succeeded in convincing many of the public that British Rail were proposing to take away all guards, including those from Inter-City trains, trains going through country areas, etc. People wore button saying 'I want a guard on my train.' They used cases of attacks on women to make the point that protection was necessary, ignoring the fact that it was not proposed to remove guards from trains with the small compartments seen on Southern Region stock and that the driver-only operated trains would be very well lit and with open plan coaches.

Legislation was used to get the guards to ballot, but there was a good deal of unofficial action before that. On ScotRail the situation was potentially very serious indeed, because the Strathclyde Passenger Transport Executive had made it clear that they would withdraw their funding – approximately £28 million – from ScotRail services in the Greater Glasgow area. Chris Green made a number of statements to the press and television in which he made it clear that he was determined that the system would not be destroyed by a few militants. It was also made clear that if the signalmen came out in sympathy, as they had threatened to do, then management would work the boxes; they had indeed done just that in an earlier local dispute.

When Glasgow Central station guards went on strike, some of

their jobs were transferred by ScotRail to Carlisle. Arranging this loss of jobs was not easy; some people regarded it as an empty threat, but the threat was carried out. As a way of making sure that the unions knew about this, the brother of a local trade union representative, who worked in the diagramming office, was used to prepare the diagrams for the transferred work.

Glasgow Central was the worst affected by the strike, and it was also the place where the worst intimidation of non-strikers took place. The unions lost the ballot nationally, and lost it in ScotRail also; and the introduction of the new trains is proceeding without complaints from the customers.

What are the principles underlying the successful management of this potential disaster? There are three clear lessons:

(i) in the beginning, the guards' leaders were skilled at whipping up feelings amongst all the men and the customers. And the system historically did not help by assuming that talking to the union leaders was the only communication method to the staff, rather than establishing a chain of communication with the men themselves. Things started to improve as soon as the British Railways Board accelerated the process of direct contact between the men on the ground and their own immediate bosses. We have already mentioned the use of the direct 'hot line' for people to ring up and talk about their fears and worries. One union leader was heard to say: 'The trouble is that the damned management are talking direct to our members and telling them what's going on.'

(ii) nobody on the management side told lies, or made empty threats. The figures which were produced showing the effects of the change on jobs, and the effects of the strike on future funding, were factually correct. The threats of job losses were carried out – the jobs from Glasgow Central have been permanently lost to Carlisle; the guards at Motherwell who blacked the movement of coal have lost 75 jobs, permanently. In an earlier guards dispute, John Clarke, the Area Operations Manager at Motherwell (known to everybody as 'Big John'), was stopped by a picketing guard as he entered his office. 'After this lot's over you can stand on your head and whistle out your arse,' said Big John, 'but you won't get your job back.' He didn't.

(iii) the negotiators hung out for a solution that could be implemented. No hiding behind words that were so ambiguous that they pleased both sides; it is in the very nature of that ambiguity that each side understands something different by those words, and this difference becomes apparent when the solution comes to be implemented.

THE POLMONT DISASTER

In July 1984 an express train between Glasgow and Edinburgh was derailed through striking a cow which had strayed onto the line. Thirteen people were killed, and more injured. It was British Rail's worst accident for many years.

The cow had got onto the line through a fence which had been vandalised; local people used to break it down in order to create a short cut over the railway line. The fence had been mended twice that week already – once earliery that same day.

There are approximately 100 cases a year of trains striking large stray animals. The Polmont case was a genuine freak; because of the lie of the land – it was in a steep cutting – the first coach derailed, went up the bank as if it were a ski ramp, and landed on its back on top of the second coach, which was where most of the casualties occurred. A train coming in the opposite direction stopped just in time, due to some extraordinarily quick thinking and skilled handling by its driver.

There is a practised drill for railway accidents. The emergency services were on the scene within minutes. A diversionary route for other rail traffic was quickly organised. John Boyle, the Director of Public Affairs, had just driven to Blackpool for the family holiday; he heard the news on the radio and turned round to drive straight back again. Volunteers manned the ScotRail House switchboard. The local pub took in casualties, making them comfortable and letting them phone home (some were foreign tourists). The manager of the pub, the Answer Inn at Polmont, would not accept any money for this, but later on there was a social event to thank him at which a collection was raised for his favourite charity. Significant help was also provided by the immediately adjacent Polmont Young Offenders Institute.

There are two immediate tasks following such an accident: looking after the injured and the relatives of the dead, and investigating the causes of the crash to see what lessons can be learned. Senior ScotRail managers visited all the injured in hospital. Then the task is one of settling compensation; here it is a pleasure to mention John Biggs, the Claims Officer at the British Railways Board, who is a very skilled and sensitive person. He sees his job as a customer relations task first and foremost; it is not his task to distribute railway resources unthinkingly, but he sees every claim as an opportunity to turn an enemy into a friend, or at least to behave with understanding and humanity in a difficult situation. The British Railways Board admitted liability immediately, and the claims were settled as quickly as possible; if there are any outstanding, it is because claimants' solicitors have introduced delays. Contrast this with the appalling length of time it takes to settle claims for medical negligence; injuries in traffic accidents; injuries to airline passengers.

The procedure for investigating railway accidents is, as we have said, so open that cover-ups are not possible. And the recommendations are mandatory, to a mandatory time-scale.

There were three factors which needed investigation in the Polmont accident: the vandalism which allowed a cow to stray onto the line; the effect of striking the cow; and the use of push-pull train sets in which the locomotive pulls the train in one direction and pushes it for the return journey. The train concerned was being propelled from the rear and driven from the leading coach. It was not at all clear whether the push-pull feature had an effect on the accident; the evidence was equivocal. Similarly, it was not clear whether cow-catchers would not cause more accidents than they would prevent. Many tests have followed to ensure that those deflectors provided on the Edinburgh–Glasgow line meet all the criteria of safety and that those being provided for future BR stock will be effective in all conceivable circumstances.

For several years ScotRail have been running anti-vandal trains; trains that look like ordinary DMU's (diesel multiple units), but equipped with special facilities and with policemen on board to catch anyone trespassing or seen doing damage to trains, track, or people. To date 2,500 vandals have been caught; but the deterrent effect must be even greater – imagine the effect if you were getting on with some happily mindless vandalism only to find a train-load of fit policemen disgorging from that innocent-looking DMU you were planning to damage.

Another answer to lineside vadalism is better fencing. Here there is a dilemma and a cost problem. It is not legally allowed to have a fence on railway property covered in anti-vandal non-drying paid (the sort that sticks to your clothes and hands) or with razor tops, because an innocent passer-by who just felt like hopping over the fence would injure himself. So the fences have to be doubled, with the real protective fence on the innner side; which greatly increases the cost. Nonetheless, this has been done in some locations. And no opportunity was lost to bring it home to local people that loss of life at Polmont was due to vandalism.

Other improvements to safety included the speeding-up of the introduction of radio communication to all trains; this was in the plan already, but delayed through technical problems, cost, and some initial difficulty in getting union acceptance. The need is now clearly seen and radio signalling in different forms to meet different needs is being implemented fast. But we are now at the stage where most railway accidents are attributable to sheer human error, frequently a combination of the errors of two separate people: a failure of vigilance, a confusion of messages, a laspse of attention. Vigilance tasks are very difficult to research properly; the evidence suggests that for someone to concentrate on a single display (such as a radar screen, or an airport security screening device) and report no false positives and miss no real positives he must take a break as frequently as every twenty minutes or so. Railway workers do not work in such

High speed train in Fife

unstimulating and lonely conditions as radar operators, but the problem of keeping concentration is obviously bigger and more difficult than the lay person would imagine. Tests of personality and other factors may help; ergonomics has a lot to teach us. But human error in perception or judgement can never be completely eliminated. And in practice the way the railway industry is likely to go is for systems which are largely automatic and which give an alarm if something goes wrong – or if an intruder crosses some location – so that the operator only has to use the display as an exception.

There are two points to add about the Polmont accident. One has to do with the handling of the media. In older days the railway representatives at the site of an accident were virtually forbidden to talk to the news media, pending an inquiry. They are now allowed to give more facts, if these are readily evident, though not of course to indulge in blame or wild speculation. This has gained them much more understanding treatment from the news media themselves.

The second point has to do with the speed of implementation of changes recommended by the investigation – or even before, if it is obvious that something has gone wrong which can be put right. With very few exceptions, the changes are implemented fast. Compare this with the record of the airlines in implementing safety measures: for example, it has been known for years that many people in air crashes survive the crash but parish from asphyxiation due to burning upholstery. Nothing was done about this; in August 1985 55 people lost their lives when a British Airways plane caught fire on the runway at Manchester Airport. The same upholstery is still being used. The time to clear an aircraft is still tested using fit people in overalls in an empty plane; not mothers with babies, and elderly people, struggling through hand baggage and duty frees. It is possible to react quickly to safety recommendations even when the bureaucracy makes reacting to almost anything else impossibly slow. And if the railway can do it, why can't other organisations?

Disasters are not the most pleasant way of learning what people are capable of. But they are an opportunity to learn, and to weld the team together. Shared trouble and tragedy has always been part of the railwayman's experience, just as it is that of the miner and the sailor. The important thing is to learn enough not to have to face the same disaster twice.

9 · Teamwork

One of the first things that strikes a visitor to ScotRail is the nature of the teamwork at the top. Valerie Stewart first noticed it in a meeting where three of the four top team were present. Each of the other three went to some trouble to represent the point of view of the absent member, even when they all knew that he would be saying something different from all of them there. This was so unusual compared with many other organisations that she started to study it further.

Then she picked up a couple of other clues. One was hearing Vivian Chadwick discussing his relationship with Chris Green. 'Chris builds things with things,' he said, 'and I build things with people.' It was indeed a true reflection of how they interacted; Green never happier than looking at an old station and dreaming up plans for refurbishing it, Chadwick never happier than when plotting some new way of busting the bureaucracy or enabling people to do their jobs better.

INTERACTION

The second clue lay in the amount of informal interaction within the top team. The top four at the time – Green, Chadwick, Jim Cornell and John Boyle (Director of Public Affairs) – developed strong personal relationships with each other and with the rest of the ScotRail team. There were many social events which cemented the teams together. One got the feeling that these were people who liked one another as friends and would seek out one another's company no matter what organisation they were working for.

People working together in a group can either enhance one another or get in one another's way. We choose task forces or working parties because we believe in something called synergy; we come back from work grumbling about having spent all day in meetings and achieving less than we could have done solo behind the desk. It's painfully obvious that some groupings of people work well, and some are disastrous.

(*top left*) Chris Green, General Manager, ScotRail, and now Director, Network South-East; (*top right*) Jim Cornell, Deputy General Manager, and now General Manager, ScotRail; (*bottom left*) John Boyle, Director of Public Affairs, ScotRail; (*bottom right*) Vivian Chadwick, Regional Operations Manager, ScotRail, and now Deputy General Manager

As part of the research for this book, Valerie Stewart asked all four members of the top team to fill in a personality questionnaire (the Myers-Briggs Type Indicator, or MBTI) which is particularly good at revealing why people get on, or don't. She then fed it back to them. The results, and their comments, provide a good deal of insight into why the ScotRail top team is greater than the sum of its component parts.

First, what does the MBTI measure? It looks at how people come to decisions – how they get information, where they get information, how they decide what's important, and their preference as between taking decisions and gathering information.

EXTRAVERTS AND INTROVERTS

So, the first of its four scales determines which of two possible worlds the person gets their information and energy from. There is the outer world of things and people, and the inner world of ideas. This represents the technical distinction between **extraversion** and **introversion**. In terms of behaviour, **extraverts** tend to like variety and action; like to get on with the job; tend to be faster and impatient with complicated procedures; dislike long slow jobs; are good at greeting people and like to have people around; don't mind the interruption of the telephone, or working in a noisy office; and are relatively easy to get to know. **Introverts**, xy contrasts, tend to like quiet for concentration; tend to be careful with details and don't mind working on one project for a long time; want to know about the ideas and principles underlying a job before getting on with it; are content to work alone and may have trouble remembering names, greeting people, or working in noisy offices with a lot of interruptions; and are relatively difficult to get to know.

In common parlance we used these terms to indicate sociability or withdrawnness. This is not the way they are used here; it is possible to be quietly interested in things and people, or noisy about ideas. And the concept of extraversion-introversion, like the others used here, are not either-ors but more like handedness; every extravert has some balancing introversion, and vice versa.

SENSING AND INTUITIVE

The second scale of the MBTI concerns how people access their data, from whichever is their preferred world – the external or internal. There is the style which is dependent on the use of external data as evident to the five senses; and the other style, which gets data using the sixth sense – not dependent on any external reality, but on an 'aha' or a 'what if' which comes out of the blue. These two styles are called **sensing** and **intuitive**. **Sensing** people tend to be rooted n the here and now, and in the past. They like details and established routines, and are impatient when the details get complicated. They seldom make errors of fact, and are good at precise work; they work steadily, with a realistic idea of how long the task will take. They distrust inspirations – their own or other people's – and dislike new problems unless there are established ways of solving them. They comprehend a situation one step at a time, and may have trouble seeing the big picture; they often like absorbing facts for their own sake. **Intuitive** people, by contrast, are future-oriented; they dislike doing the same thing over and over again, and prefer learning news skills to using them. They like new problems and new ways of solving old problems. They follow their inspirations, good or bad, and often make errors or fact or jump to conclusions on the basis of very little data. They are not so good jt precise work; they work in bursts of energy with slack periods in between. They comprehend a situation by looking for the underlying pattern, the skeleton, the complexities, and may have trouble noticing the details.

Extraverts outnumber introverts by three to one in the general population. Sensing types outnumber intuitive types by a similar ratio. So, if you have followed the outline so far and think that you are an introverted intuitive and have felt in a minority all you're life – you're right.

THINKING AND FEELING

The third distinction drawn by the MBTI concerns how people decide what is important, having got their data from whichever is their preferred world and through whatever means they prefer. One style – the **thinking** style – decides what is important according to qhat is scientifically correct and analytically true. The other style – the **feeling** style – makes the decision according to what will promote harmony, make people feel good, or conform to the person's own ethical values. **Thinking** people are relatively unemotional; like analysis and putting things into logical order; settle disputes by appealing to objective criteria. They can get along without harmony, and may hurt people's feelings without noticing it; they need to be treated fairly, and can fire or reprimand people where necessary. **Feeling** people, by contrast, tend to be very aware of other people and their feelings; like pleasing people, even in small things, and are sympathetic. They like harmony and can get upset by office feuds or having go give people had news. They need the occasional spot of praise. They settle disputes by appealing to harmony and human values. It is not the case that thinking people are unemotional toughies and feeling people are nice warm cuddlies; some of the most caring working environments are provided by strong T-people, because it makes sense to be nice to people; and Hitler was almost certainly a strong F, because he made decisions according to his own values, which happened not to be very nice.

The T-F distribution is roughly equal in the general population, but far more T's than F's find their way into business and industry.

PERCEPTIVE AND JUDGING

The final differentiation concerns whether people would rather spend their time in the data-gathering mode (the **perceptive** type) or in the decision-making mode (the **judging** type). **Judging** types live according to plans, objectives, and schedules; they like authority, structure, and accountability; maintain standards; are best when they can plan and follow their plan through. They may decide things too quickly, or be reluctant to change their plans when new information comes in. **Perceptive** types live according to the moment and adjust easily to the unexpected; they need autonomy, variety, and stimulation, and dislike being held to plans and objectives. They are irreverent towards authority. They are good at adapting to changing situations, though they may leave things for too long before acting; they often need to create some pressure before they will actually deliver.

Like the T-F differentiation, the J-P distribution is equal in the general population, but there are far more J's than P's in management jobs.

From these four pairs of letters come sixteen possible

combinations: each set of letters indicates a particular type. For example, an ISTJ is an introverted sensing type with thinking and judging. An ENFP is an extraverted intuitive with feeling and perception. The different types show clear differences in behaviour; in the kind of jobs they are attracted to; in the people and ideas they find congenial; in the things they find stressful and the way they react in stressful situations. Many signalmen, for example, are ISTJ's: they are happy working alone, prefer to concentrate on the details, want them logical, and have a preference for following a plan. Many of the best communicators are ENFP's: they are interested in people, have a sense of the overall picture and what will happen next, like to please and entertain people, and can adapt readily to changing situations. Most of the world's brilliant scientists ure INTJ's; their intuition feeds them ideas which they judge according to logic and wish to see worked out in the outside world.

The MBTI was devised by an American lady, Isobel Briggs-Myers, and members of her family and associates. She had two items on her agenda: she had worked with young people and was concerned to ensure that people went into jobs which would not force them to work out of their weaker side. And she had a deep dislike of the conflicts people get themselves into, and wanted to find ways of getting people to use and value the differences between people rather than making the assumption 'Not like me = bad.' Many of the conflicts people experience can be illuminated by looking at their type differences. For example, sensing types may regard intuitives as head-in-the-clouds, airy-fairy, unrealistic, slapdash, given to firing off mad ideas without thinking them through; intuitives may regard sensing people as stodgy, uninspired, down-to-earth, backwards-looking, and too concerned with detail. Judging types may regard perceptive types as aimless, frivolous, changing with every wind, promising more than they can fulfil and unnecessarily irreverent to authority; perceptive types may regard judging types as stodgy, authoritarian, slow to change, too committed to their plans and the status quo.

Yet wherever there is conflict between people there is the opportunity for complementary. One person's weakness is the other person's strength, if only they can come to regard it so. The ScotRail team covered just about every option from the four MBTI differentiations, and used these differences in a constructive rather than destructive fashion.

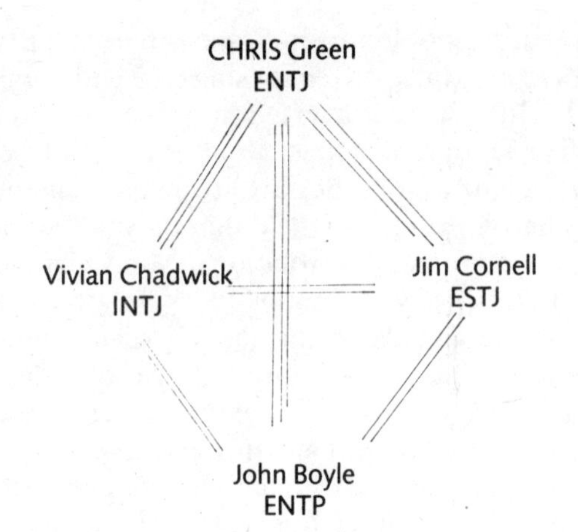

Fig 5 The team at the top: Complementarities

From the diagram a number of things are obvious. We have three extraverts and one introvert. Three intuitives and one sensing. All four are thinking types, but in three the T score was not very strong. And there are three judging types and one perceptive type.

What does this mean in practice? Let us look first at the four people and see what the MBTI theory would have to say about each as individuals:

Chris Green is an ENTJ. ENTJ's have very strong natural leadership qualities. They have bounding enthusiasm which carries people along with them even though the way ahead may not be clear. They have a strong drive towards mastery; towards truth and justice; towards reform of phe inefficient or illogical. They set themselves long-term goals and mobilise energy – sometimes in apparently incredible amounts – towards achieving them. They are change-oriented, and their intuition gives them not only a vision of the future but also a comprehension of the leaverage points for changing it. They have little tolerance for dependent relationships; they can be incredibly patient when explaining to other people how to get help, but very impatient when the other people apparently prefer helplessness or failure; they prefer to be offered solutions rather than problems.

Jim Cornell is an ESTJ. ESTJ's have an enormous respect for logic, analysis, efficiency. They organise facts and situations well in advance and make systematic efforts to achieve their plans and objectives on schedule; they are happy giving orders and seeing that the orders are followed through. ESTJ's are realistic, matter-of-fact, common sense people. They are not usually instigators of radical change, but once convinced of the need for it will implement it with close attention to the details, and their commitment to hard work means that it is difficult for them to give up or to tolerate failure.

Vivian Chadwick is an INTJ. INTJ's are the most self-confident of the 16 Myers-Briggs types, and very single-minded. They live in the world of ideas, focussing on possibilities, and they want to see these ideas logical and worked out in practice. They are natural decision-makers, looking to the future; they are builders of systems and appliers of theoretical models. While no idea is too far-fetched to be considered by an INTJ, they quickly discard ideas or systems which do not serve a purpose; thus in an organisation they will rebel against unhelpful rules and bureaucracies, seeking all the time to establish structures which enable rather than restrict necessary change. Like ENTJ's, INTJ's have strong leadership qualities; but they tend to be best at leading people who are already committed, and less interested in leadership tasks where first the people have to be converted. They can be demanding and difficult to satisfy; dislike small talk; and do not suffer fools gladly.

John Boyle, the Director of Public Affairs, is an ENTP. ENTP's are enthusiastic innovators, always seeking new ways of doing things, new projects to undertake. They are confident of the value of their inspirations; tireless with the problems involved; and ingenious with any difficulties which occur. They are always looking for a better way of doing things – and some better = new; and ENTP's dislike of routine is very strong. They drive other people very hard, though they often need pressure themselves before getting things completed – ENTP's are often found burning the midnight oil on projects which should have been completed weeks before. They like complex situations, particularly complex people situations, and so are at home with politics and political intrigue. They are often charming people, good communicators – particularly when seeking support for new ideas – and fun to be with. Their perception makes them extra-sensitive to changes in the external environment, and they react quickly. They are not the world's best planners; for them it is more important to do things, improvising if necessary, than it is to sit and plan how one will do things.

The complementarity in the team should be apparent. A team

composed totally of intuitive types would be very change-oriented, looking towards the future, energetic and improvisatory; the balancing sensing type (Jim Cornell) will make sure that the intuitives' ideas are sifted to see which are practical, and the detailed plans put into operation to fulfil the ideas. A team composed totally of extraverts would pay attention to the external realities such as re-organising the infrastructures, recruiting support from other people, etc.; the balance introversion (Viv Chadwick) makes sure that attention is paid to the management system and structure, and to the underlying principles. A team composed purely of judging types would be very good at setting objectives, making plans, having things ordered and disciplined; the balancing perception (John Boyle) will draw their attention to those circumstances where the plans need changing, the objectives restructured, the success criteria altered.

The only function not represented amongst the four top team members is the **feeling** function – the preference for making judgements according to what specifies personal values and promotes harmony rather than according to what is logical (the **thinking** style). However, thinking types are not necessarily ignorant or careless of other people's feelings; they respect and care for people's feeling because it makes sense to do so, rather than just because it gives them a nice warm glow themselves. And all four of the top team have a very strong concern for people, as individuals and as groups.

Between them the top team (seen here before Chris Green left for the South) encompass just about every function that top managers need to perform: The General Manager as commandant, visionary, leader, enthusiast; the Deputy General Manager as realist, implementer, consolidator, planner; the Regional Operations Manager as a different kind of visionary, bureaucracy-buster, change agent, creator; the Director of Public Affairs as communicator, politician (using the word in its constructive sense), provider of new ideas and sensor of the first signs of change. The differences are used in a complementary fashion, not as a source of dispute or dislike.

Of course, any organisation is composed of many teams. We have looked in detail at the top team, but each person there is leader of his own team, and the same principle of complementarity often (not always) applies. For example, it is difficult for an INTJ to devote much time to the management of the here-and-now; they are much more interested in creating new ideas for the future. So Vivian Chadwick created a Current Performance Manager post; someone to pay single-minded attention to the management of the daily performance of the railway. This change supports not just the personalities involved, but also the nature of the job; a Regional Operations Manager ought to be planning for the future, but it is easy to get drawn into the daily problems. An ENTP is not the world's best planner; John Boyle has working for him people whose job it is to translate his ideas into actions.

Chris Green has now gone to the London and South East Sector (recently restyled Network South East) as Sector Director, and Jim Cornell is now General Manager, while Vivian Chadwick is Deputy General Manager. The major task facing ScotRail now is one of consolidating the ground already gained, and making sure that the enthusiasm and commitment generated in the early days of rapid progress are maintained as the organisation changes to reflect the needs of firm business orientation, and then – hopefully – a reasonable period of stability. Who better to do this than an ESTJ consolidator, implementer, who will work ideas through to completion? Vivian Chadwick's replacement as Regional Operating Manager is Jim Summers, an ISFJ. ISFJ's are exceptionally good at reading how other people are feeling; want a smooth-running organisation and contribute hard to achieve that aim. They are realistic, hard-working, and dependable; not pushy, and therefore often under-valued. Thus the top team has changed slightly; a bias towards consolidation, a strengthening of concern for people, just as the task demands; but each member of the Curry Club, as the top four, much to their discomfort, became known, and the many other senior managers who were less keen on curry but just as involved in the team from which we have here taken a small section, and who are all equally importantly ran their own teams in their own way to achieve the goals of the Railway will surely carry for a long time the memory of working in a group of people where 1+1+1+1 = 5 at least.

10 · External Relations

In an organisation like ScotRail it is vitally important to maintain the goodwill of the local community. They are the customers; in some cases they are the sponsors. If they like their railway they will do a lot for it; if not, they withdraw support.

It is also important to have good relations with the other railway Regions and with the British Railways Board. To some extent we have told the ScotRail story as if it were an independent business; in part this is justified because of its geographical and economic separation from the rest of the railway, but we could be judged to have ignored two important elements: the successes and failures of other Regions, and the contribution of the Board. In a way, it is like talking about one subsidiary of a holding company.

So, in this chapter we look at some of the more important relationships which ScotRail must sustain in order to keep successful: with customers; with local and national government bodies; and with the British Railways Board.

CUSTOMER RELATIONS

Customers first (as indeed they should be). The Central Transport Consultative Committee is a national body with branches at local levels (Transport Users' Consultative Committees), implemented by Act of Parliament in 1947 as a way of channelling complaints and suggestions to the railway. They will take up complaints from an individual customer, or look at overall railway policy. In the past, the TUCC has been pushed into a rather backwards-looking role; investigating complaints, publishing an annual report detailing the railway's failures. It has no authority to contribute to policy on a local or national level.

Chris Green involved the ScotRail TUCC in decision-making, rather than complaints handling. Their Chairman, Colonel Bill Dalzeil, is basically a strong supporter of good public transport – this helps. There were a number of occasions when the help of the TUCC was sought in the planning stage and contributed usefully.

Members of the TUCC came to customer first conferences – an exercise which strengthened relationships on both sides, as the TUCC saw how hard the staff were trying, and the staff saw that the TUCC were not ogres. Bill Dalzeil was the real originator of the £10 voucher scheme which instantly rewards excellent service.

There is always a danger that committees of consumers become biased. For a start, there is a 'professional consumer' type known to every nationalised industry and government monopoly; middle class, often female and articulate. Another source of bias is that such committees tend to attract only those people who can afford to spend time on them: retired people, people who run their own business, senior managers who can get time off for 'community service'. Ordinary working people often have neither the time nor the experience – nor in some cases the belief in the value of their own views – to think that such service could be open to them.

To counteract this danger, many Area Managers started their own consumer panels. Memberships of the panel was usually by invitation; for a fixed period only; and with a conscious effort to counteract the bias towards the professional consumer. For example, the Area Manager at Glasgow Central has on his panel the Area Customer Service Manager, the Assistant Chief Constable of the British Transport Police, a member of the Scottish TUCC, two commuter travellers, one Inter-City traveller, and the Travel Centre Manager. He consults them on a regular basis about issues such as vandalism and security; new station developments; industrial disputes; Travellers-Fare services; and the promotion of tourism.

Having this regular contact with consumer groups does a number of things. First, it gives ScotRail some ambassadors in the local community; if they understand more ubout what the railway is trying to do they can explain it better to their colleagues and friends. Second, it changes the relationship from an adversarial one to a consultative and information-sharing one. Third, it provides a source of data which railway people might miss, because however hard you try if you have worked in one industry for years it becomes difficult to look at it completely objectively. There is not a lot one can do in the short-term to implement some consumer suggestions – for example in the spending of capital sums – but many of the smaller things such as minor timetable changes, different cleaning patterns, better information, etc., can result from customer suggestions. And of course the practice of ringing up a customer who complains rather than send a written reply gives another source of useful information.

Many local communities in Scotland must have thought that the railway had forgotten them. The old grey station, where the centre of the town used to be but is no longer, with never a lick of paint or a hint of attention to customer comfort . . . it's a part of history, but not necessarily a part of one's daily life. Two or three major initiatives were started to put this right.

PRESENTATION

First, the intensive programme of station refurbishment. Starting with the major stations and going on so that almost no station in ScotRail is untouched, the stations were completely re-done. Of course, many of the buildings are listed and cannot just be torn down and re-built. But within these constraints the Architect's department did a magnificent job.

How was this accomplished in so short a time, particularly when there was a prevailing atmosphere of gloom and pessimism, a belief that we were stuck with the stations as they were? It was another exercise in busting the bureaucracy, of course. Jim Cornell, who as Depury General Manager was responsible for the investment budget, gave some principles:

(i) Use simple construction methods, local materials, and simple designs.

(ii) Try to get the design right first time and commit to it, instead of chopping and changing after the design has been put to bed.

(iii) Don't go for the cheapest solution but the most cost-effective and appealing one; and take into account, under the term **cost-effective**, what will appeal to the customer as well as to the engineers.

(iv) Think about maintenance at the time of designing, not later.

(v) The bureaucracy would say that every contract has to be examined with a fine tooth-comb. Go out for competitive tenders, have all the options analysed. This can take too long. Go instead for contractors whose work has been satifactory in the past and whose skills are known.

(vi) Delegate a lot of the work to the Areas. They know what is needed better than Head Office, and have a vested interest in supervising the work to completion.

(vii) Commit publicly to given finishing times, and keep to them.

Any design is a compromise between Aesthetics, Function, and Buildability. Perhaps too much emphasis was given in the past to the latter two criteria, so that one got buildings which looked minimalist; which had perhaps started as cost-effective and finished up by looking just plain penny-pinching. There were two new factors in the ScotRail design philosophy; one, that if you build in aesthetics from the beginning then it costs no more to build a pleasant-looking building than an ugly one; and second that there are perhaps many uses which buildings are put to which have not been made clear in the specification. We have yet to get right the ability to build buildings which are completely easy to maintain; for example the new Operations Depot in Edinburgh looks superb, the exterior being clad in glass, but nowhere in the original design are there any means of cleaning the said glass.

Much effort was put into getting the local communities involved with their stations. You can do a lot with opening ceremonies and celebrations. John Boyle, who must know every newspaper editor in Scotland, did a great job ensuring media coverage and the involvement of local firms. Sometimes the involvement was unorthodox; the station at Lochiel was built as a project by the local Outward Bound centre, with ScotRail engineers in supervision.

Not just stations but whole lines have been built or improved. The Edinburgh Bathgate line was re-opened to passenger traffic on 24th March 1986, 30 years after its pre-Beeching closure, using funds which had come from the EEC, the Scottish Office, Lothian Regional Council, the District Councils and ScotRail.

RELATIONSHIPS WITH LOCAL AND NATIONAL GOVERNMENTS

Another way of getting local involvement and acknowledging local support is by the naming of locomotives and trains. There have been 33 locomotives-naming ceremonies, including power cars, in the past two years. Whether it's a famous name or a local personality, the ceremony will draw in the crowds and help maintain contact with the community: in January 1986, for example, Mrs. Shand-Kydd, mother of the Princess of Wales, named a locomotive *Ben Cruachan* at the ceremony to mark the completion of rebuilding of Oban Station. In all there were 70 public events within 6 months during 1985, compared with eight in a comparable time before Green became General Manager.

And when the event included giving hospitality to important visitors, these visitors found themselves with hectic schedules and constant attention: Jimmy Allan, Area Manager Edinburgh Waverley, recalls' Mr Green's secret was – don't let them loose too long by themselves. Hence the early breakfast meetings and the late evening tours. The need to impress the opinion formers was ever present in the new style.'

Some of ScotRail's funding comes from the national government through the Public Service Obligation (PSO) system and some from the European community. On a more local level, a sizeable sum comes from the Strathclyde Passenger Transport executive; some from the Scottish Development Department of the Scottish Office; and some from bodies such as the Highlands and Islands Development Board. Although the Conservative Government is publicly reputed to dislike the railway industry (Mrs. Thatcher has rarely been able to travel by train since she was elected, partially because of the security problem) many of the ministers have been more than sympathetic and helpful. Peter Parker asked for the railway to be judged according to performance criteria as well as by purely financial criteria; but in order for the shareholder to do this the shareholder must understand the nature of the business as well as the balance sheet. It is a tribute to David Mitchell, who was the Under-Secretary of State responsible for the railway for much of the time when ScotRail was going through its turn-around, that he took a lot of trouble to really get to know the business for which he was answerable to the Prime Minister. Valerie Stewart recalls waking up on a train from Cornwall once to find Mitchell – whom she did not recognise – working on his papers opposite. They got into conversation without revealing their identity; she was very puzzled as to the identity of this stranger who was singing the praises of ScotRail while wearing an Inter-City 125 tie. Once all had been revealed she was immensely cheered to find what an understanding Minister the railway had, and how broad was his knowledge and commitment.

A serious charge that can be levelled at many of this country's financial institutions is that the paymasters and shareholders do not understand the business. This leads to them judging the value of the business on inadequate parameters: they look for short-term profit, and not at the long-term survival prospects of the business. They can therefore sell out too soon or lose confidence in other ways, when a business is going through minor problems.

In take-overs and mergers their attention focusses on what the acquisition will do to the balance sheet and not what it will do for the business. Top managers spend too much time shouting about how good they are, and not enough on getting better. Though the railway has only one shareholder, the principle applies: the more intelligently the shareholder understands the business, the more constructive in the long term the relationship will be.

RELATIONSHIPS WITH THE EUROPEAN ECONOMIC COMMUNITY

Relationships with the European Economic Community are also important. Much of Scotland is a development area, entitled to receive EEC funding which may be as much as 55 per cent of any particular project. Maybe the 'auld alliance' between Scotland and France helps, too. As an example, the new training centre at Rutherglen costing approximately £900,000 was built with partial EEC and MSC funding. Other examples of projects which have been supported with EEC funding are: the Ayrshire Electrification (Route Rationalisation and Resignalling) scheme – 30 per cent of the total, amounting to approximately £8 million; (ii) the Yoker Resignalling scheme, for which the EEC are paying 50 per cent of the costs; the Yoker EMU carriage Depot, the Queen Street–Cowlairs Resignalling Scheme, amounting to about £10.5 million in the years 1985/87. £300,000 came from the EEC to the Bathgate line. And the Ardrossan–Largs electrification scheme has been allocated a 50 per cent grant, amounting to £1.5 million.

Much of this money is not discretionary; it has only to be applied for in the right way, and this is one of the areas where perhaps the rest of the railway does not do as much as ScotRail to get funds. The task of liaison with the EEC is achieved in ScotRail by allocating one person full-time to relations with the EEC.

Relationships with other Regions and with the British Railways Board are important. In the worst case, ScotRail can be as good as it possibly can, but if the rest of the railway is dreadful nobody will use it to come to Scotland from the rest of the country. ScotRail interests with the rest of the system on at least two levels: the operational level and the managerial level. On the **operational** level, the performance of ScotRail trains is affected for good or ill by the performance of the Midland and Eastern

Regions who feed it with long-distance Anglo-Scottish trains, and vice-versa. The sleeper attendant who brings you your early morning tea at the wrong time of arrival in Edinburgh may be based at King's Cross. During late 1985 the Midland Region in particular was having severe operational problems and these pulled down ScotRail's figures. Design decisions are sometimes taken nationally for the good of the whole railway which might not be perfect for ScotRail or indeed for other individual Regions. Sometimes the reverse is the case, as when the Western Region chooses an alternative method of signalling without radio different from the one piloted in ScotRail, at apparently less cost but less efficiency. There are always decisions about which Region or Business shall be chosen to receive new investment, or to try out high-quality innovations. Decisions on personnel and industrial relations matters are taken nationally and sometimes reduce the freedom for individual Regions to do as they would prefer: for example, ScotRail would like to offer more employment in some rural areas where the contribution of the individuals would be uneconomic if they were employed at the basic rate. If they could be employed at a lower rate of pay or part-time it would be better than being on the dole, and better for ScotRail, but not possible with the present national system.

Managerially, when one subsidiary of a larger organisation is doing well there is always the prospect of synergy and the prospect of envy. ScotRail tries to manage for synergy; there is nothing to be gained by puffing one's own successes at the expense of one's colleagues. Chris Green made no secret of the fact that he plagiarised many of his best ideas from other organisations or other Regions – often his success lay in the speed and thoroughness of their implementation rather than in the ideas themselves. The best ideas, and the mistakes, have been shared with other railway managers. Most of the other Regions have plagiarised the ScotRail carriage cleaning methods, for example. Most of them now have a Current Performance Manager in the Regional Operations Manager's office – a ScotRail idea which was happily made available. Most now have Area or Regional Customer Care Managers, under varying titles – another ScotRail idea. Some have adopted the idea of Area Business Groups: a delightful example could be found on the Cotswold line from Oxford to Gloucester, where the Area Manager, David Mather, was given authority to spend more money than Area Managers usually have to smarten up stations, start local marketing initiatives, etc.

Sometimes the plagiarism fails. We can give two examples: the Ullswater courses and the fate of Cornish Railways. In 1985 Colin Driver, who was then Deputy General Manager of the Eastern Region, asked for some courses for his supervisors like those run by ScotRail at Ullswater. Valerie Stewart explained that the prime purpose of these courses is organisational development, and they are for building teams of independent people who – amongst other things – return motivated to start busting their bureaucracy. Driver, who also has little patience with bureaucracy and understands the investment that organisation development work requires, concurred. However, he then left to become Director of Freight, so the courses were without a top management patron. The first course therefore failed to meet its objectives: the participants arrived thinking that they were going to learn outdoor skills (one participant, asked what he had learned on the course, responded by saying that he would now be able to shin up signal gantries better); the review, which was intended to make the bridge between managerial lessons learned on the course and the managerial situation back home, was conducted by a young Area Manager (supervisors who have come up through the grades see young graduate Area Managers as part of the problem, not part of the solution); he of course could not deliver on the kind of changes to the system that they had identified as necessary, nor could he talk authoritatively about policy. And when they came back for the review they said that the operational situation was so bad that they were spending all their time fire-fighting and could not get the support for the improvements they wanted. The course was not repeated.

The second example of failure in plagiarism is that of Cornish Railways. Cornwall is like Scotland in that it is geographically and spiritually seperated from the rest of the British Isles; economically depressed; and with its railway permanently under threat. Its Area Manager was Rusty Eplett: another 'character' whose attitude to rules and bureaucracy was to look for the best ways of bending them in favour of his own business objectives. Rusty was another of those who knew all the staff by heart and had their loyalty. He conceived the idea of Cornish Railways and started to give it the same local identity and pride that ScotRail has; not on the same scale, because he was operating as an Area Manager rather than a Regional Manager, but on the same principles. For reasons of administrative ecomomy Cornish

Railways is now run from Plymouth (you will never get a Cornishman to admit that Plymouth can understand its problems) and Rusty was retired early and with some acrimony on both sides.

PLAGIARISM

It is worth taking time to look at the principles of good plagiarism, considering the way lessons are interchanged between ScotRail and the rest of the railway. For instance:

(i) when borrowing an idea, look at the reasons for which it was introduced. If your reasons are different, think again. Not merely because operationally the idea might not work out as well, but because the staff may think that your reason is the same as that of the source. Taking away barrier staff from some stations, for example, may begin as a way of reducing jobs and taking out of the public gaze people who are not good at cusomer contact. But another Region may use the idea as a way of improving revenue, by simultaneously strengthening ticket checks on trains. It will be seen as a job-cutting measure the second time around, not as revenue-improvement measure.

(ii) when borrowing an idea, look at the managerial reasons and principles underlying it. The experience of the Eastern Region with the Ullswater courses is a good example of this. Getting a better way of monitoring carriage cleaning is not good unless you also borrow the management principle that people are dedicated to particular stock and have to go back over their own mistakes. Getting a better way of monitoring telephone answering is no good unless the supervisors have authority to move resources until the performance is up to scratch.

(iii) when borrowing an idea, look at the resources needed to implement it. If customer care training takes three days, do not automatically assume that it can be done in two.

(iv) when borrowing an idea, ask if people need training to use it. ScotRail pioneered the use of briefing groups in the railway, and made sure that managers were trained to operate them. Other parts of the railway, and many other industries, have tried and failed because of lack of training and back-up facilities.

(v) when borrowing an idea, ask if its speed of implementation is part of the reason for its success. Area Business Groups succeeded in ScotRail not merely because for the first time Area Managers were allowed to submit proposals for investment, but because their proposals got a quick response. The speed of response but it had a

> much more important effect on the morale of the people involved. All the Regions have customer care courses in which the staff are invited to make plans for doing things better, and asked to put their questions directly or (more usually) indirectly to management. Some of the Regions get the answers back to the staff within days or weeks. One has taken eighteen months. They might as well not have done it at all.

What about relations with the British Railways Board? The ScotRail experiment could not have started, let alone succeeded, without the commitment and support of the Chairman and his executive. If there is tension in the system, it comes from two sources: the inevitable – hopefully creative – tension between production managers and business managers (i.e. the General Mangers and the Sector Directors) and between specialist functions in the Regions and the specialist functions at the Board. These things are only to be expected and are the experience of any big organisation where the top team are committed to change but the commitment does not always filter easily down two or three levels to the specialists. Green used to capitalise on the Scottish dimension as much as possible in his relations with Board: having a British Railways Board meeting at the Caledonian Hotel, he arranged for haggis and a piper – the complete works. Someone suggested that some people did not like the pipes. 'Nonsense,' retorted Green, 'that must be some damned Englishman.' He understood perfectly the Scottish dimension as well as the national dimension.

RELATIONSHIPS WITH THE PUBLIC

The art of good public relations is, of course, to establish the relationships when times are good so that they are there to support you when times get hard. During the 1985 guards' strike there was probably more public concern than criticism of the railway in Scotland, even though the long-suffering customers went through weeks of disruption. When the public are basically favourably inclinded they will support rather than criticise. It is doubtful whether, if the old atmosphere of uninterest or hostility had still prevailed, the head of ASLEF in Scotland would have felt able to speak out as he did against the strike; it was a courageous act by Johnnie Walker, which helped to convince the public that the railway unions were not all composed of mad hot-heads.

Good public relations also has an effect on the staff. The 1985 ScotRail Review published in Modern Railways went to all members of staff. There was hardly a word of criticism about the money spent (it cost £16,000 to produce, as opposed to the £20,000 which had been spent on a previous communications exercise of lower quality). The publicity gives them something to live up to, and makes them feel that management trust them enough to tell the world that they're proud of the service. There was some criticism from some members of staff that maybe Chris Green had too high a public profile, but this was a deliberate ploy in the early stages of the regeneration; it is easier for everyone – staff and customers – to identify with a person than with a system. This high profile for the General Manager was later toned down and more effort given to make the Area Managers and the other senior officers visible to the customers and staff. There is a good parallel in the military world, where a leader will rally his dispirited troops by putting on his medals and visibly bringing himself to the front of the column; not because the leader needs the trappings of status, but because he recognises that the troops need a figurehead.

But the best public relations in the world will not cover up for a bad product. There is a fine line between shouting about your existing achievements in order to get support for more, and shouting about them when they are only half-done. Sometimes the staff felt that the public profile was a bit too optimistic, when they knew how tightly the service was managed. But the PR machine has never been brought in to tell lies or to cover up for mistakes.

Some priciniples therefore of ScotRail's public relations efforts:

(i) Establish relations before you need to call on them in times of trouble.

(ii) Informal relations are just as important as formal relations, with everybody – staff, individual customers, and organisations.

(iii) Invite the views of the customers and concerned organisations, and don't think that 'professional customers' are telling you everything you need to know. You need access to the gossip network, both to give and to get valuable information.

(iv) A high public profile associated with one person or a small group of people may be a good thing, but only if that person or people is prepared to live up to the demands this will make on him or them.

(v) Don't promise things you cannot deliver.

(vi) Don't tell lies.

(vii) From time to time, do good by stealth.

(viii) Don't ever allow yourself, publicly or privately, to see the relationship as adversarial or manipulative.

(ix) Don't use the P.R. machine to cover up for failures in the product or service.

(x) Never forget that the best P.R. comes from individual members of staff who are proud of the service they work for. The General Manager can be a figurehead, and he can create the climate, and he can do these things well; but the customer sees the travel clerk or the ticket examiner and takes his view of the service from these.

To finish, two personal stories. John Boyle saw a station supervisor being rude to a customer. The incident happened two days before a big station opening, but it became his number one priority and that of the Regional Operations Manager; it was dealt with the following day. Not by issuing written notes through the system, but through direct personal action. Excellence in small things needs close personal attention.

The other is a Chris Green story. He was travelling to the re-opening of a previously closed station at Loch Awe, which he was due to open. On the train he found himself in conversation with an old lady who could remember being in service at the local great house in the days when the station was still operating, many years ago. So, when he got to the vital part of the opening ceremony he asked the old lady to step forward and open the station in his place – and her name is now on the commemorative plaque.

11 · What Next For ScotRail?

It is difficult to draw a line in the history of an organisation and say: this side of the line is past, and this side future. As this book is being completed, it is late in 1986. Many things will change between now and its going to press; many more will change after its publication. So it would be unwise to give a long list of predictions which will either be history or hostages to fortune.

We are glad that the succession was assured before Chris Green went to work on Network South-East. Thus, though the details of the journey are unknown, the leadership is assured. We do know that whatever the business priorities of ScotRail may be, the unforgettable lesson is that achievements in business depends upon the hearts and minds and skills of everyone in the organisation. To this end, the one enduring priority of ScotRail will be its people. Everything that can be done will be done to increase the authority, confidence, and ability of the staff at all levels. There are some Victorian values which we can do without: chiefly the distinction between 'wages grade' and salaried staff, though it is not possible to say when this target will be achieved. In future ScotRail may employ fewer staff, but the ones it has will be more skilled; better trained; and enabled to make the best possible contribution to their industry and their Country.

Before we go on to the second part of this book, which is about applying the ScotRail lessons in other industries, just one or two pictures from memory:

> A (non-railway) visitor from South Africa who was so impressed with the stations on ScotRail that he insisted on visiting every station within ten miles of his holiday itinerary.
>
> A group from the Ullswater courses, who had never abseiled before the course, abseiling down the 10-storied ScotRail house to raise money for local charities.
>
> The joke people told about Chris Green: that at the funeral of a colleague he had gone up to the grieving widow and taken her by the arm, explaining that while she probably felt dreadful now, he could

assure her that time heals all wounds, that one day she would notice the sun shining again, that she would smile again, '. . . and I give you two weeks to achieve this.'

And the other one: that at the time of the guards' strike Green was using the media so much and so skilfully that Terry Wogan was trying to get on the Chris Green show.

And a quote from a guard who didn't know that he was talking to the author of a book about ScotRail: 'In the old days, you used to be a bit ashamed to say that you worked for the railway, because everybody got at you for dirty trains, late trains, strikes, that sort of thing. But since all this began, I'm proud to say that I work for ScotRail.'

And, just in case you were wondering about the bottom line of punctuality, some figures:

1984

	On time Per cent.	On time or less than 5 minutes late Per cent.	Over 30 minutes late* Per cent.
Eastern Region	73·8	89·2	3·6
London Midland Region	79·9	90·4	3·4
Western Region	64·3	82·1	3·0
Southern Region	76·1	92·0	1·1
Scottish Region	84·7	91·2	4·5
WEIGHTED TOTAL	77·0	90·5	2·8

* Class 1 trains only (that is, all inter-city services, Scottish express services and some long distance provincial services).

1985–86

		Trains arriving	
		on time *Per cent.*	*on time or less than 5 minutes late* *Per cent.*
Eastern Region	Class I	52	71
	Class II	73	90
London Midland Region	Class I	53	68
	Class II	77	88
Western Region	Class I	60	77
	Class II	72	90
Southern Region	Class I	65	85
	Class II	75	93
Scottish Region	Class I	65	77
	Class II	89	93
Weighted Totals	Class I	60	77
	Class II	77	91

Class I trains include all inter-city services, Scottish express services and some longer distance provincial and London and south-east sector services.
Class II services comprise all other passenger services.
Statistics Courtesy of British Railways Board

12 · Could the ScotRail Solution Work for You?

In the rest of this book we look at how to take the ScotRail lessons and apply them – if they fit – to other organisations. Not every organisation needs the ScotRail solution, so we begin with some diagnostics directed towards telling whether your organisation is experiencing the systems crisis – the problem of drowning in one's own rules and bureaucracy, needing something different in order to come through the transition, but not being sure qhat the medicine is or how to take it.

A spot of revision. The **systems crisis** is that stage in the growth of the organisation where the systems and controls that were brought in earlier in order to correct the disorder which happens when a pioneering organisation gets bigger, themselves start to take over, slow things down, over-centralise, become too bureaucratic. Thinking about your own organisation, go through the following check-lists:

PIONEERING STAGE

The Pioneering Stage has the following characteristics:

– the founder is still around and has close personal control of the business

– the number of employees is relatively small

– communication between employees is fairly informal

– there is little or no attention to rank and status

– there are few, if any, specialists around, other than those necessary to running the core of the business

– there is a general atmosphere of 'mucking in', everybody doing whatever jobs come to hand and need doing

– it is difficult to predict the demand for the organisation's products or services

In the pioneering stage, the agenda for the organisation should be to get the best out of that stage and build strengths which can be drawn on to aid the transition for the crisis. Hence the advice often offered to small business to be rather more systematic about finance than many of them would be out of normal inclination. Hence also the advice to get more specialist help than they feel they need: a good accountant, a good marketing or publicity adviser, sensible business record-keeping. It is also important to recognise that just staying small will not stave off the pioneering crisis for ever: at some point the pioneer may feel the need to sell out or to hand on to his or her progeny, and a successful pioneering organisation is always vulnerable to a take-over bid.

There are examples aplenty of good pioneering organisations, though few of them become national names while they are still in the pioneering stage. Many of the business media run competitions or offer awards for successful new businesses. The corner shop; the software designer; the dress designer; the recruitment agency . . . the list goes on. One very interesting way of being a pioneer while remaining protected from the crisis is the franchise system, which has enabled lots of people to start up as caterers, printing shop owners, dry cleaners, etc. MacDonalds will ensure your product quality, train your staff, do your shop design, and advertise for you, while you do the best you can to cook the hamburgers and bring the customers through the door. An alternative to the franchise system is the 'licensed dealer' method, whereby a manufacturer sells through a limited number of retailers whose standards he attempts to guarantee through training and other forms of quality control.

The Pioneering Crisis usually has a selection of the following characteristics:

- the pioneer himself leaving, through boredom, death, or take-over
- the organisation growing to a size where the pioneer can no longer communicate with everyone on an informal, day-to-day basis
- an increasing need for the pioneer to spend time on administrative and financial matters rather than on developing the main activity of the business
- a cash-flow crisis, brought about perhaps through recklessness with the money earned in the first flush of success, or through difficulty in predicting demand for the company's products, or through bad debts and slow payers

– the need to go to the bank to fund investment to make the organisation bigger, if the bank makes demands for a rather more structured way of running the business than heretofore

– a threatened take-over or merger

– the entry of competitors into the market, if they learn from the pioneer's mistakes and are able TO PRODUCE A BETTER PRODUCT AND GET IT ONTO THE MARKET QUICKLY

– in certain cases, usually in computer technology, the difficulty of selling a product whose price is falling at the same time as the market is getting more demanding and the amount of dealer and manufacturer support required is increasing

The way not to handle the pioneering crisis is by more pioneering behaviour, i.e. by running around inventing things, making a public spectacle of the pioneer's charisma, etc. Unfortunately this is just what some organisations do, and by so doing only make the crisis worse. One or two examples:

The BUPA organisation started its centre for preventative health screening under the aegis of Dr. Beric Wright, an undoubted pioneer. He persuaded various organisations to put up the money for a centre in London, initially at the Institute of Directors and later in the King's Cross area. The nature of the service was dictated by Dr. Wright, who had fairly fixed ideas about what constituted good screening practice. The service was expensive, selling to the wealthy and worried well. And it came very nearly to disaster, for the following reasons:

– little or no control was exercised over the chief providers of the service, i.e. the doctors who conducted the consultations. Though they were supposed to consult in a certain style and take a given length of time over doing so, there was no attempt to enforce these standards.

– the service was expanded to a size where it was difficult to maintain informal channels of communications, including opening branches in other cities within the UK, but few attempts were made to provide stronger and more formal channels.

– no attempt was made to adapt the service offered when competitors came into this apparently lucrative marketplace. For example, one potential corporate client was able to specify, using its own company medical officer, what screening tests were necessary for its particular purposes; this request was rejected, and the client went elsewhere.

– poor sales and after-sales support meant that the number of corporate clients was not as great as it perhaps could have been, and the return rate of individual clients was very low.

The organisation responded initially not by doing the things it should have done to improve the basic service, raise staff morale, and increase sales, but by bringing back the pioneer out of retirement to run things. This did no good at all. Only late in the day did they turn to the proper solutions to the pioneering crisis, i.e. improving the organisational structure, exerting more control over the quality of the product through the use of quality circles, etc., and adapting their services to meet the threat of competition.

Other examples of failure in the pioneering crisis are usually part of the experience of anyone who tries to buy a new house. It seems to be an inescapable part of the game that small builders are under-capitalised, disorganised, bad at controlling their workforce, poor at communicating with staff, customers, or the necessary utilities, and given to muddling through and paying attention to whoever shouts the loudest. Because they are selling a commodity that nobody can do without, many of them stay in business who would doubtless go to the wall if they applied the same techniques in any other industry.

SYSTEMS STAGE

The Systems Stage, which comes as the necessary answer to the pioneering crisis, has the following characteristics:

- formal planning and control mechanisms, for budgeting, work-flow, human resources, etc.
- the division into line and staff functions, and maybe the development of a Head Office and separate divisions
- often, mechanisms such as Management by Objectives and related disciplines
- personnel management schemes such as job evaluation, performance appraisal, career planning
- specialists and specialist departments on the pay-roll

Because much of this book is about organisations in the systems crisis, we do not want to give the impression that systems are themselves a bad thing, or that any organisation in the systems stage should be looking to get out of it at the earliest possible opportunity. There are plenty of organisations in the systems stage which are very profitable and should stay there for as long as is necessary. Sainsbury's, for instance, is just such a business; a highly planned, very centralised, controlled, low-risk organisational style is exactly what you need when your major task is to do more cost-effectively tomorrow what you did yesterday. It would be silly for Sainsbury's to attempt the kind of strategy which worked for ScotRail, because they do not need it; though any organisation in Sainsbury's position should be constantly monitoring to see whether the controls that are necessary to running the business are from time to time stifling people's initiative. Almost any single-product extractive business, to take another example, will be in the systems stage and needing to be there; and as long as they watch to see that their markets are not being taken by competitors and that their labour relations have not become formalised to the point where the union is effectively in charge, then that is where they belong.

We write as if organisations were single, unitary phenomena. Rarely is this the case. If people are asked to diagnose where their own organisation fits on the corporate growth curve, many people in big organisations draw a distinction between the organisation as a whole and their own division or department; often they say that their division feels at a younger stage of growth than the whole organisation, particularly if the business consists of a number of different products or activities. This can be just an interesting part of life's rich tapestry, or it can cause real problems if you have sub-sections of the organisation coming up to their pioneering crisis just at the time that the rest of the organisation is entering the systems crisis. However, we suspect that for many businesses one recipe for success is the overseeing by a systems-stage Head Office function of a mix of activities, some of which are in the pioneering stage and encouraged to behave in that way. In Marks and Spencers, for example, the central central functions of the business are conducted in a highly systemised and planned way but there is a fair degree of freedom to take risks in product innovation.

The Systems Crisis usually has a mix of the following characteristics:

- decisions take a long time to get made
- decisions are low- rather than high-risk

– there is a great deal of management by committee, and very little opportunity for the individual to achieve on his or her own

– communication with the workforce is through the union, and only through the union

– specialists are dictating too much the activities of line managers

– functions that belong with the line management, e.g. quality control and labour relations, are formally or *ipso facto* delegated to specialist departments

– inter-departmental feuds and rivalries are commonplace

– managers' freedom to respond to commercial necessties is restricted by rules and regulations which cannot be bent, or bent in time

– more energy is spent in managing the boss, Head Office, and 'the system' than is spent in managing the staff or responding to the needs of customers

– the customers are shown the rule-book rather than treated as people who have choices

– the customers start to leave, or in the case of a monopoly organisation, they form pressure groups to persuade the organisation to become more responsive to their needs

– the lost business goes to smaller, nimbler competitors

One very important thing to remember about the systems crisis is that its early signs are often difficult to detect from the top or even the middle of the organisation. The first signs are usually internal – the slow decision-making, the difficulty of taking risks, the in-fighting between departments. In firms which have large numbers of customers rather than two or three big ones dealt with at top level, the early signs of customer desertion are more visible to the people on the periphery, because they are the ones who have to deal with the customers. In too many organisations the early signs of the systems crisis are ignored at the top, or the senior managers adopt a style of 'don't tell me the bad news' and so the necessary action is delayed until things become serious and the stock market starts to sell the shares.

There are plenty of examples of firms in the systems crisis to be found in the recent history of British industry. In the car industry, for example, British Leyland showed many of the signs a few years ago: talking to the workforce through the unions, letting the customers do the product testing, over-specialisation between departments and inter-departmental rivalry, the reduction of managerial authority and the reduction of risk-taking. The high-street revolution in department stores is knocking our many of the old firms whose systems and controls prevented them from responding quickly to market changes: Debenhams fell to the Burton Group, which was itself deep in the crisis before it was rescued by Halpern. The legal profession is probably still in the crisis; small attempts to break the monopoly of various parts of the profession on various legal services are slowly, so slowly, bearing fruit.

We suspect that the reason why so many big firms are in the crisis now or just coming through it is a combination of historical accident, the kind of people who get drawn into organisations at the start of the systems stage, and their response when under threat, thus:

The major industries in the UK, with very few exceptions, had to start over again after the Second World War. Thus their experience in the 1950's and early 60's was that of the pioneering stage; in a market anxious for consumer goods, they did not have much cause to examine their management style or structure. In addition, as Corelli Barnett points out in his book **The Audit of War,** the fact that the UK is rich in natural resources probably deluded many earlier managers and proprietors into thinking that their rather laid-back and reactive style was in fact the best possible way to manage. Other countries, with fewer natural free gifts, had to develop more managerial skills to compensate.

In the early 1960's the problems of growth brought these industries into the systems stage. Those of us who were around then can remember the alacrity with which solutions characteristic of the systems stage were adopted by many big UK firms – for a while it seemed as if you could not meet a group of managers anywhere without the conversation drifting towards discussion of Management by Objectives systems, or the best way to organise corporate planning. The systems themselves were necessary; but organisations in the early part of the systems stage also attract into them people who are good at the planning and controlling style of management. In terms of the Myers-Briggs Type Indicator, which we discussed in Chapter Nine, they are typically people with the -SJ style: **sensing**, i.e. paying close attention to detail, good at applying past experience to new problems, and *judging*, i.e. wanting to have things planned, controlled, and orderly. The -SJ style is naturally conservative and tends towards the bureaucratic; dislikes ambiguity; and gets the best results when they can plan their work and follow the plan. So, in the early stages of the systems stage, we suspect that organisations attracted a great many -SJ types, who learned that the way to be successful was to specify and apply the plans and the rules.

Twenty years on, what happens? The organisation is perhaps heading towards the systems crisis; the -SJ managers are now at middle or senior level; and their response to the crisis is to apply their past experience to the new problem, i.e. to strengthen the rules and controls. For many firms in the systems crisis, one major problem is this layer of 'corporate concrete' at middle and senior manager level; the people on whom salvation depended twenty years ago, the people who ingested the idea that there was a clear way to be successful in the organisation, the people whose naturally slow and cautious response to change is taking away the organisation's chance of survival into the next stage. What is to be done with them? The organisation owes them a moral debts, but carried to excess their style will ensure that the organisation cannot progress further. It is a major management development issue for the next decade.

ScotRail gets help from all sorts of sources. Sister Mary Ross, well-known in Scotland for her work in psychological counselling, helped on one of the Ullswater courses, where we take the participants through the model of organisational change and ask them to guess where ScotRail lies on the growth curve. Mary's comment when she saw it: 'That's just like our Order. Our older Sisters entered when the main task was teaching, and they are usually strong on the need for control and order – in other words, -SJ's. Now the work is much more with problem families, or in social work; most of the younger vocations are -NF's (the intuitive feeling type, the people who place the most stress on harmony, understanding, authenticity). The -SJ's are now in positions of authority, and their high need for control and for repeating the procedures of yesterday is interfering with carrying out the new mission. But how do we cope? In a commercial organisation you can at least hope that your corporate concrete will retire some time, but our Sisters are with us for life, and we are bound to them in charity.' It is not merely yesterday's solutions that need to be jettisoned in the systems crisis; sometimes it is yesterday's people also.

INTEGRATED STAGE

The Integrated Stage, for the few firms who have really got there, looks like this:

- decentralisation of control from Head Office towards the divisions, and within divisions to the lower levels
- an increase in authority given to junior managers
- a conscious attempt to make it easier for people to take risks
- a move to get back closer to the customers and give them what they want
- communication with the workforce through more direct means, rather than relying on formal relations with the trade union
- the re-emergence of the charismatic leader
- breaking down of inter-departmental boundaries and rivalries
- a move towards the introduction of enabling systems
- making line managers more responsible for issues that had previously been handled centrally, e.g. day-to-day industrial relations, quality control, etc.

We said that few firms had actually made it into the integrated stage. Those that have are commonly quoted as examples of corporate turn-around: British Airways, British Leyland; or as examples of organisations that somehow manage to adapt their style of whatever the current needs are, e.g. ICI, IBM. So, to predict (as we are sometimes asked) what lies ahead of the integrated stage, or what the integration crisis looks like, is not something we can do. Our major purpose in this part of the book is to try to draw out the lessons from ScotRail – an organisation well and truly in the systems crisis – and offer them to firms in the systems crisis or coming up to it.

At what stage do you diagnose your organisation to be? If you are in the pioneering stage, then the ScotRail lessons are not for you – yet. Read in order to see what's ahead of you, so that you may plan for it and meet it with strength. If you are in the pioneering crisis, then get yourself some simple, robust systems; simple systems introduced early, while you still have room to maneouvre, will do better than the sort of system you need to manage, a complex and mature crisis stage. And be aware that you do not recruit too much potential 'corporate concrete' to help you out of the difficulties.

If you are in the early part of the systems stage, plan to have a good one. Get yourself systems that are really relevant to your own organisation – to its size and time-scale, to the people involved, to its customers. Don't collect information you don't need. Don't try to control the things you don't need to control. Don't impose the full weight of the bureaucracy on those parts of the organisation that may still be in the pioneering stage. And set up methods to ensure that the systems crisis, when it comes, is spotted early and navigated through with skill. (The methods, incidentally, are more likely to involve 'management by wandering around' than they are to involve committees and check-lists).

And if you are in the systems crisis, or moving into the integrated stage but unsure what it looks like, read on: see how the ScotRail experience organisation can help you.

13 · Leadership

We have already said that one characteristic of the integrated stage – one of the factors necessary to come out of the systems crisis – is the emergence of the charismatic leader. The reason for this is simple: that the only certain thing in the systems crisis is that things cannot go on as they are, and a new success formula is necessary. Someone therefore has to take responsibility for saying to the people who form the organisation: 'Follow me. Put your hand in mine and together we'll go somewhere different. **Where** we're going I'm not quite sure yet, but we have to make a start.' And in order to get people to put their hand in yours and follow you into the dark, they have to trust and believe in you. You do not earn that trust by learning lots of management techniques, or by going to business school; you do it by being the kind of person that people would, quite simply, die for.

We do not intend to get drawn into the debate about whether leaders are born or made. In this chapter we discuss how you recognise the charismatic leader (though they usually stand out for themselves); how to develop leadership characteristics within an organisation; and what factors within the organisation will support or inhibiit the growth of leadership within it.

CHARACTERISTICS OF A CHARISMATIC LEADER

What, then, are the characteristics of a charismatic leader?

First, they are *future-orientated* rather than backwards-looking. True leadership uses all the skills available to command the future. The thinking of a charismatic leader constantly grasps for the intuitive logic underlying what is known, or can be guessed, about what is to come; and then seeks for the most cost-effective route through the logic to the desired outcome. This speed of thinking, and constant search for pattern, often passes for instinct or luck; to a person who is happier to do a critical path analysis, spelling everything out on paper, this style of thinking can look suspiciously like 'winging it'.

Winging it – going into situations unprepared and relying on being able to think fast on your feet – is not however a characteristic of the charismatic leader. The real leader puts a great deal of effort into absorbing information, and is distinguished by *open-mindedness* and an ability to **listen** to information, regardless of source. The manager who protects himself against unpleasant information; who gets his information from quasi-military tours of inspection at which the troops stand by their beds and shake their heads silently when they are asked if they have any complaints; who never asks the customers what they think of the product, or tells them that their complaint is in fact unjustified: he'll never make a leader, because the people he would like to lead know that going into battle on insufficient information is likely to lead to disaster.

Openness to information is important. The information can come at any time of the day or night: Valerie Stewart was just going to sleep on the sleeper from Edinburgh to London when she recognised the voice of the person being checked into the next compartment – Chris Green. She popped her head out to say hello and was immediately drawn into a discussion on what needed to be done next for the railway. In this the two of them were shortly joined by a customer on his way to his night-time ablutions, who had a complaint about the service. You have to get the picture of Chris Green in a business suit, Valerie in a Victorian nightie, and the customer in Harris Tweed overcoat from which protruded bare and hairy legs disappearing into black boots, standing in the corridor putting the railway to rights. You never know when you may learn something.

This story illustrates also the **energy level** needed to be a good leader. Leaders start early and finish late: not because they can't delegate, not because they get themselves into messes that only they can get out of, but because of the sheer fascination of, and commitment to, the work they do. They tend to assume that other people have the same energy level also (which can be a bit hard if you've just set your heart on a spot of well-earned shut-eye).

And – and this is important – they can switch off and relax. The difference between the person who works hard because he can't keep up with the demands of the job and the person who works hard because he loves it is that the latter knows that good self-management means keeping yourself fresh for the task. It's not uncommon for the charismatic leader's form of relaxation to take the form of another kind of work; you're unlikely to find them slumped in front of anything that happens to be on the television. But it's the change of pace, and the change of focus, which is important.

Another important personal quality is **courage**. The ability to go into a room full of angry strikers; the ability to go into tough negotiations; the ability to face tough interrogators from the media, to speak up for an unpopular proposal in the conviction that it is right, to defend an unpopular decision once taken . . . hhe physical, moral, and intellectual courage of the true leader is unmistakeably. It is seen most clearly in the military, where one contrasts the 'leaders' staying behind the lines in their chateaux in the First World War with the true leaders, many of them unrecorded, who were there in the trenches with the troops. Courage respects the courage and efforts of others: Wellington could afford to call his troops 'the scum of the earth, enlisted for drink,' but Nelson couldn't, being on the same ship.

Charismatic leaders have **values** which they bring to their work, and encourage others to bring to theirs. They do not usually trumpet them from the hill-tops; only when you have been working with them for a while do you discover a deep commitment to honesty, to the fulfilment of human potential, to a strong moral and ethical stance on the things that really matter. It is of course possible to have a commitment to values that are really rather nasty – Ayatollahs are charismatic too – but it is difficult to command that 150% commitment from other people if your major value is seen to be just that of making lots of money, or knocking the opposition out of the sky.

Leaders in action have three clearly outstanding features:

First, they prefer to win co-operation rather than demand it. They will demand if they have to, but they know that one volunteer is worth ten pressed man. They know that if you demand people's co-operation you then have to spend energy on enforcing it; they would rather it were given freely. This costs them energy, and time taken in getting commitment; more importantly, it costs them the constant expenditure of psychic effort involved in trusting people and being trusted. When you work for a charismatic leader, you are aware (unless you have given him good cause to believe otherwise) that he trusts you. And for him to trust you costs him the constant awareness that you may betray that trust; yet he would rather it were so, because when you act to control someone you put a limit on what they can achieve, but when you trust them then you make it possible for them to give their best.

True charismatic leaders share another characteristic in action: they **choose good people** to work for them. Ideally, they will appoint people better-qualified than they. They are not afraid of the possible threat of being outstripped: 'If Joe can do the job better than I can, then he ought to have it,' is what they say when someone points out that by appointing Joe they might be doing themselves out of a job. You will not find a true leader surrounding himself with place-men who mean no threat. Nor will they stand in the way of their subordinates' development.

Finally, to steal a quotation from Robert Townsend's *Up the Organisation:* 'You can always tell a good leader because one way or another his subordinates always turn in a superior performance.' Though there is the story of the orchestral conductor (now forgotten) who was to conduct the Vienna Philharmonic one evening and at rehearsal chose to harangue the players about Mozart's exact intentions when writing a particular passage. The Vienna Phil are rather good at Mozart, and resented the upstart's lecture and his conducting style. After a while, the leader of the orchestra came up to him and said in a sibilant whisper: 'Listen. Any more of this from you and . . . we play it the way you want it.'

You are running a large organisation moving, you hope, into the third stage of development. You think that you have some young managers with leadership qualities further down the structure. What do you do to enable those qualities to develop in time to let you retire peacefully?

HOW TO DEVELOP LEADERSHIP QUALITIES

Leadership does not grow by spoonfeeding. Developing leadership qualities in another person is much more a matter of giving them the necessary resources to develop for themselves than it is about the formal, trainer-led teaching you would get on a management course.

Vital for the development of leadership potential is the **opportunity to command** at an early stage in one's career. It is often better to give the young leader a small patch to call his own than to make him a small fish in a big pond. Valerie Stewart helps some organisations in their graduate recruitment programme, administering psychological tests. One candidate, in a transnational organisation, showed in the tests and interviews that he was an outstanding natural leader. Her advice: for goodness sake put him as soon as possible to running a small overseas operation. Unfortunately other considerations prevailed; he spoke fluent German, and the organisation was short of German speakers, so he was assigned to the Frankfurt office where he was one of 20. He left within eighteen months.

One of the finest young leaders we have seen – Andy Guthrie, in the ScotRail British Transport Police – sighed with relief when he was taken away from the acting rank as second-in-charge and put back to his substantive rank. Sergeant Guthrie said: 'Thank God I'm back in charge of my own patch. You can't change anything when you're only second-in-command.' Leaders need to be able to change things; it's part of their driving force. They develop the ability to put this need into practice when significantly encouraged by their boss – as Andy has been by his Assistant Chief Constable Archie MacKenzie.

Though we suspect that the experience of command is more important than the absolute size of the task, another crucial part of the leader's development is the **challenge of the task.** One difficult task makes more contribution than seventeen easier ones all at once. The leader needs, like a test pilot, to be 'pushing back the envelope' of what's possible. The best developmental tasks are often multi-disciplinary, where the leader who has trained as a scientist has to concentrate on people, or the leader who began life in finance has to get the best out of technical specialists. 'I had to go and close down a factory,' said one young leader. 'Everything – the financial forecasts; the local authorities and politicians; telling the workforce and the mangers; selling the site and the equipment; fixing the re-training, the counselling, the social security for the people we were putting out of work. I was appalled at first, and I hated it, but it was one of the best things that ever happened to me.'

It helps the development of leadership skills if the young leader can himself **work for other outstanding leaders**. A spot of hero-worship does nobody any harm, and learning about leadership at second hand is no substitute for seeing it in action. The sheer invigoration of good leadership is good for the morale: Valerie Stewart remembers the start of some current work for the National Health Service. The NHS since the Griffiths Report has become the honey-pot for all sorts of consultants and all sorts of packaged solutions; it is badly managed, and from time to time extremely depressing. I was walking back from the Harrow Road

Clinic in Paddington, having seen squalor and indifference on a scale I never thought to see, and was seriously wondering whether there was anything I could do to help. I couldn't find the button to press to start to make things better, and I was damned if I was going to be just another leech feeding off the moribund body. Then I thought: 'Chris Green wouldn't walk off the job,' and I squared my shoulders and started swinging my briefcase again.

Send your potential young leaders to work for other charismatic leaders. The senior manager, if they are the leader you think they are, will not resent the younger person nor see them as a threat; the work of making tomorrow better is never finished, and a true leader will modestly and honestly pass on his skills.

Your young leader will make mistakes. The man who never made a mistake never made anything. And if you don't make mistakes, you don't learn. The young leader needs support in recovering from these mistakes; counsel rather than interrogation; help in seeing what went wrong and planning to recover; help in putting things in perspective and regaining one's sense of humour. The young leader may need to feel that his boss is publicly proclaiming his trust in him. Only when the young leader fails to learn from his mistakes should the support be withdrawn.

The young leader also needs the **resources** to do the work assigned. This is not an argument for giving him a blank cheque; it is an argument for saying that the leader should have some say in choosing the most vital resources to work for him, particularly the people. Chris Green has now gone to become Director of Network South East; he took with him Ronnie MacIntryre, the architect who has transformed so many of ScotRail's stations, because the job there was too urgent to spend time negotiating a new relationship with new architects: he wanted to work with at least some people who knew his way of thinking. A good leader will often turn around a poor performer, so we are not arguing for never giving the young leader a recalcitrant team; just saying that you cannot make silk purses out of sows' ears.

In big organisations, particularly those with technologies or customer bases which are highly specialised, young leaders often benefit from a programme of **secondments** or contact with outside industries. You can be easily seduced into thinking that your own firm's way of doing things is the only possible way; to see how other people do it is very instructive. The railway style used to be very much one of sending people on instructional visits to see other railways in action, but rarely to look at other industries; when we started to visit some High Street stores to see how they managed, our perspective was radically altered. This of course is the theory behind Action Learning – the programme of planned secondments and job-swaps pioneered by Reg Revans and used by many organisations in the UK and overseas. A thorough Action Learning programme has the advantage that it also builds in a network of young leaders who can support each other through the hard times; in an organisation going through massive changes, this networking idea is worth picking up for its own sake, to let the young leaders share their experiences and hopes.

Finally, on the topic of developing young leaders, a couple of strategic points:

First, the young leaders can come from anywhere. They are not necessarily found through the graduate recruitment programme, or through the formal management development process. They may be people who are exercising their leadership abilities outside work because discontent with the bureaucracy has led them to stifle it between nine and five; the people who put a lot of energy into the local community, into youth work, into voluntary work. Nor are they necessarily chronologically young; an organisation in the systems crisis often stifles the leadership talent amongst its middle managers and its specialists, and there may be good material there, as well as in the under 35's.

Second, do look to see if your organisation encourages people to specialise too early, and makes it difficult to cross divisional boundaries after a limited time. We have seen far too many cases of people with natural leadership and general management abilities prohibited from moving as they should into more general management posts because they specialised early and now lack the necessary technical competence to manage credibilly all the functions they would have to as general managers. This is particularly the case, in our experience, with scientists and engineers, who may lack finance and production experience and so have to stay in their specialist stream at a cost to them and to the organisation. Also, it is too often the case that the best specialist gets promoted to being the leader or manager, when in fact the more cost-effective solution would be to keep him as a super specialist and bring in the best manager as leader.

MOTIVATION

Finally, how to reward and motivate your young leaders? The most important source of motivation for many of them is just the ability to be able to accomplish things; to change the world and see that it has changed. Money is not neccessarily a motivator, but the unskilful misuse of money can be. In other words, your young leader may work for very little himself if he sees that the work is useful and that other people are similarly rewarded; what galls him is the sight of other people in the same industry being paid more for less. It is certainly not the case that monetary reward has to be equated with performance; some of the finest leaders we know work in poorly-paid industries – but fairly-paid industries.

One important source of motivation for the young leader is the kind of feedback on performance that allows him to point to something tangible and say: 'I did that,' or 'I had a hand in that.' It's the feeling you get when you sit on a hill above Bristol with a manager from the water industry, and see if his expression of quiet satisfaction as he looks at the city – which looks so small you could hold it in the palm of your hand – and know that he's thinking that none of the people there could go about their daily life unless he did his job well. You get the same feeling with a lot of railway managers standing on a busy station in the morning peak, or watching a load of aggregates commencing their journey: a contentment in having had a hand in something visible. You see it in someone like Paul Wyatt, Industrial Relations Manager for Reuters, who has put more effort than most people into turning around poor performers, and gets a quiet thrill when he hears about the promotion of someone he went to a lot of trouble to help. You see it, perhaps at a more senior level, in the faces of managers in one-industry towns when they look out of their windows at the shops and houses below and know that perhaps one income in three below them depends on how well they do their job.

We have made this mythical charismatic leader sound like a saint, and a remarkably hard-working saint at that. But saints are rare, and good leaders not so rare; it's just that somehow leadership in industry has become something in short supply. Leaders spring up in all sorts of unlikely places, and from all sorts of unlikely sources: look at the way the world responded to Bob Geldof, for example. Where there is a real job to be done, sooner or later someone will come forward to lead it; the task for all of us is to lead or to follow, as is given to us, but not by action or inaction to stand in the way.

Lao Tzu, a sixth-century Chinese philosopher, said:

> The best rulers are those whose existence is merely
> known by the people.
> The next best are those who are loved and praised.
> The next are those who are feared.
> And the next are those who are despised.
> It is only when one does not have enough faith in
> others that others will have no faith in him.
> The great rulers value their words highly.
> They accomplish their task: they complete their work.
> Nevertheless, their people say that they simply follow
> Nature.

14 · Busting the Bureaucracy

Bureaucracies help to make things predictable. They put everything in its place. Your GP does not have to work out from first principles every time he wants to refer you to a consultant at the local hospital. You know that you write to the Environmental Health Officer at the council offices to complain about the smell of the chickens in your neighbour's window-box. You know that you probably need to see a solicitor about your house purchase. In this way, a bureaucracy helps to make clear the lines of command and authority.

Unfortunately, the average bureaucracy also brings with it some problems. It is usually slow to react. Because it places particular tasks and functions in particular offices, it is difficult to remove those tasks from those offices if there is a need to cross functional boundaries or get a quick reaction. It produces the Peter Principle – that in a hierarchy every member tends to rise to his level of incompetence. It can drown itself in paper. It can submerge the talents of its employees who wish to take risks or do something different. It can get so preoccupied with its own internal purposes that it loses sight of the mission for which it was created, or the customers it exists to serve. It can become so horrendously expensive to run that it seems to be like a dinosaur, which needs to spend all its time eating merely to keep alive, and has no spare energy left for wandering around the forest.

Busting the bureaucracy takes insight; take will; and takes techniques. The *insight* is needed to see how much of the bureaucracy is necessary for the good functioning of the organisation. You do not move out of the systems crisis merely by abandoning all rules and all forms of control. In any organisation it makes sense to have some functions centrally managed: the purchase of large orders, dealing with national or transitional customers, etc. It makes sense to have some rules of conduct by which customers and employees can form their expectations of the organisation. Careful insight will show which of these rules and systems are really necessary, and which need relaxing or abolishing. On the railway, for example, we have had to continue an absolutely autocratic regard for public safety with a need to relax aspects of the bureaucracy which prevented us from responding to commercial needs, to the needs of the staff and managers, to the needs of the sponsors who pick up some of the bills.

The **will** to bust the bureaucracy is one of those things like leadership; difficult to define, easy to spot, and capable of being engendered in people who have the right basic talents through training and experience. It is difficult for a junior person on their own to set about demolishing a long-standing bureaucracy. This is one reason why in ScotRail we have set so much store on making it clear to all the staff and managers that senior managment is on their side when it comes to busting the bureaucracy; even if their attempts are from time to time clumsy, if their hearts are in the right place they will get support for their motives. The will to do these things has a number of components: a fanatical dislike of wasted resources; a belief that because things have always been so, this is no reason why they should continue to be the same in future; an intuitive sense of the pressure points in an organisation, because sometimes the best way to proceed is not through a frontal assault on the hapless bureaucrat who has stood in the way, but through a flanking movement; dogged persistence; and an ability to get real pleasure out of the thought that people you have never met are doing their jobs better because you have had a hand in unshackling them. Above all, the real bureaucracy-buster knows that you do not prune a bureaucracy merely be re-drawing the lines on an organisation chart, but that you have to enable or empower people to take the authority you are now holding out to them. To do this, the change agent will go to some trouble to create **enabling systems**.

ENABLING SYSTEM

What do we mean by an **enabling system?** Here is a list of characteristics of an enabling system, with examples:

1. All systems enforce minimum performance standards. Controlling systems effectively place a ceiling above which people find it difficult to rise. Enabling systems have a different perspective: they set a floor below which nobody has an excuse for failing. Charles Handy put it beautifully, as always, in his

book **Understanding Organisations**: that the characteristics of a bureaucracy is that it is more interested in enforcing minimum standards than in ensuring that some people excel.

It used to be fairly easy to test for this characteristic in at least one area by looking at the organisation's performance appraisal system; in a highly bureaucratic organisation you would usually find that you only got to know your appraisal rating if it was unsatisfactory, when you were probably called in for a disciplinary interview. Though this picture is itself has now faded out of most businesses (even the Civil Service now has open appraisal) you can find the spirit lives on in many other ways. For example, as a manager, is it easy to get training or development for one of your poor performers and very difficult to organise resources that will make a good person even better? Are components and supplies specified on the basis of 'what's the least we can get away with?' or on the basis of 'how well can we do for that price?'

2. The system is based on the assumption that people want to do a good job and are trustworthy. In other words, on System Y management rather than System X.

It's worth taking a little time to explain these two terms, which have got into the management jargon now and have become a little fuzzy with time. The two terms were coined by Douglas MacGregor, now sadly dead. He said that managers tend to operate on one of two theories about human behaviour at work. **Theory X** is the theory that people dislike work, will skive and get away with hhe least possible, need constant supervision and goading by carrot and stick otherwise they will not work at all. **Theory Y**, by contrasts, says that people want to work, want to do their best, can take responsibility for planning and controlling their own work, and do not need constant supervision in order to keep them trying to do better.

So far so good – and probably familiar. The most important thing which MacGregor actually said was this: that **whatever theory manager you are, your theory is self-validating**. In other words, if you behave like a Theory X manager your staff will respond in a way that suggests they need to be coerced into working at all. And if you behave like a Theory Y manager your staff will respond in a way that suggests they are capable of taking responsibility for themselves.

On one very simple level, therefore, any debate about which

theory is 'right' is bound to be fruitless, though we have sat in on quite a few. The behaviour that a Theory X manager induces in people generates the evidence that tells him he is right; and vice-versa.

Enabling systems try to encourage Theory Y behaviour; a disabling bureaucracy nearly always encourages Theory X behaviour. The transition from one style of system to another therefore nearly always brings problems; imagine a scene in which a Theory Y charismatic leader begins the process of taking an organisation into the integrated stage, and starts to put in some enabling systems. Most of the people in the organisation will have been used in Theory X style. Their tendency to respond in the style to which they have become accustomed will make it very difficult for the new Theory Y blood to succeed, at least for a while. It takes real courage and energy to manage ex-Theory X employees in a Theory Y style; sometimes the courage is needed to fire or severely reprimand an employee who will not respond. Believing the best of people and trying to create the conditions in which they can do this of their own free will is by no means an easy option.

CUSTOMER AWARENESS

An example here from Peter Argent, of British Airways, who played a part in their **People First** campaign. The check-in desks at New York were getting very crowded and it was taking too long to get passengers checking in. Queues were building up. Part of the training organisation drew up a protocol of all the stages the check-in clerks were supposed to go through; wrote it out in what they thought was the most efficient way; gave it to the clerks to go through methodically with each passenger. Peter instead took a similar group of clerks to one side; explained about the need to reduce queueing times; reminded them of the bare minimum it was necessary to achieve with each passenger in terms of administrative procedures; and asked them to use their own initiative in processing the passengers efficiently and with courtesty. This group of clerks took, on average, 25 per cent less time to process the passengers than did the ones following the protocol, and their passengers were much more likely to come away (a) smiling, and (b) understanding what they had to do next. The folk who wrote the protocol had concentrated too much on controlling the passengers and the clerks, and not enough on allowing them to use their discretion.

3. The system is expressed as far as possible in terms of principles people are to follow, not rules they have to obey. A good example of this is current at the time we write: the changing system of entitlements for Social Security payments for special needs. At the moment there is a list of benefits which people may claim as of right, or at the (usually fairly limited) discretion of the Social Security Officer. This is to be changed to a system which allows the officers more discretion and at the same time places cash limits on what they can give. Ignoring, if one can, the political implications of 'clobbering the scroungers' or 'punishing the poor', it is interesting to see how clients and DHSS officers alike are coping with the transition from a list of rules they could refer to (rules which were clear but at the same time probably gave too much to some and too little to others) to a list of principles they will have to follow.

This example illustrated another principle of good bureaucracy-busting: don't let your aims for the organisation and its clients get overlaid with a political agenda. The exercise is best done for its own sake, and explained on its terms, rather than as a political ploy or an Atalanta's apple to throw in the path of a pursuer.

4. The utility of the system is judged according to how it helps the organisation deliver a better service to the customer. One major High Street store a few years ago went in for the latest technology in computerised stock control. It involved the person manning the till in running a little electronic sensor over a machine-readable coded strip on the goods bought. Unfortunately the absolute length of time to perform this operation, coupled with the fact that the sensors did not always work as well as they should, led to the time taken to take a basket of goods through the till being drastically increased. When you have queued for 25 minutes to complete your purchase of ten buttons you make a resolution that says never again. The system is now drastically modified, but now without some complaints from those people in Stock Control and Accounts who had not been on the shop floor for a very long time and had not seen the customers walking out of the door.

Systems like this – systems which interface directly with the customer or the people who serve the customer – are relatively easy to evaluate in terms of the service improvements they provide. It is just as important to build in customer-awareness to the systems that are a long way from the customer: investment appraisal; personnel policies; project management. The system for allocating resources in the National Health Service, for example, is very rarely judged on the real quality of service it delivers to the customers; if you looked at it like a man from Mars, you would imagine that the customers are in fact the doctors, because they are apparently the ones with most say about how resources are spent. Many of the real 'customers' – who have, perforce, already spent their money through the taxation system – are spending years in pain with unglamorous conditions that present little challenge to the doctors, while resources are spent elsewhere. The Wendy Savage enquiry showed clearly that certain parts of the medical system are clearly opposed to giving the customer what she wants and will try to remove doctors who do pay attention to their patients' wishes.

COST-EFFECTIVE SYSTEMS

5. The system is minimal, i.e. it controls only those things it needs to control and to a degree of control which is cost-effective; it does not spend £1 checking whether sixpence has gone astray. Here is an example of how not to do it, given by J. F. C. Fuller:

> I hope I shall not fall foul of the Official Secrets Act if I quote verbatim the following branch memorandum. On March 10, 1926, the C.I.G.S. asked me for a pair of dividers, costing, I suppose, eighteen pence. How did I obtain them? Here is the answer:
>
> Q.M.G.9.
> 'Would you be good enough to obtain a pair of dividers for the use of C.I.G.S.?
>
> *J. F. C. Fuller,*
> *Colonel G.S., M.A. to C.I.G.S.*
>
> 10th March 1926.
>
> X Compass, shifting leg, double jointed, II.
> Q.M.G.F.(b)
> We propose to convey approval to the permanent issue of a Compass as at X above. Have you any remarks from a financial point of view?
>
> *J. Gardner,*
> *For D.A.D.E.O.S.*
>
> 11th March 1926.
>
> Q.M.G.9.(a).
> No financial objection. Would you let us have this B.M. again when the Compass has been issued?

G. Lillywhite.

Q.M.G.F.(b)
15th March 1926.

A.D.O.S.P.
Will you please arrange issue of a Compass, drawing, shifting leg, double-jointed II. to – M.A. to C.I.G.S. Room 217, War Office? Issue will be permanent.

J. Gardner,
For D.A.D.E.O.S.

Q.M.G.9.(a).
16th March 1926.

Q.M.G.9.(a).
Issue has been arranged.
I.O.P.4.D./4186 dt. 18.3.26.

H.E.,
For A.D.O.S. Provision.

18th March 1926.

M.A. to C.I.G.S.
Please let me know when the Compass is received.

J. Gardner,
For D.A.D.E.O.S.

Q.M.G.9.(a).
19th March 1926.

Q.M.G.9.(a).
Compass received, thank you.

J. F. C. Fuller,
Colonel G.S., M.A. to C.I.G.S.

How many compass stories in your organisation?

6. The minimalist structure overall is supported by checks which effectively take a micrometer slice through the organisation to see whether there are any abuses or sub-critical problems. If these are found they are corrected speedily and visibly. It is probable that the United States Internal Revenue Service collects more of the tax due to it than the United Kingdom Inland Revenue. In the USA, you fill in your tax returns at the end of the year. A large proportion goes unchecked. Of those that are checked, any found to be in default are given the kind of through going-over which leaves the defaulter in little doubt that he should have been more organised or more honest. Contrast this with the system in the UK, where in theory every return is checked but the resources do not exist to check properly (and how could they?) so that the system is based either on trust nor on fear, but on 'what can we get away with?'

MANAGEMENT BY WANDERING AROUND

Peters and Waterman publicised the phrase **Management by Wandering Around** in their books on excellence. It's easy to misunderstand which in this phrase is the key word. Some people take it as meaning that managers should take a lot of exercise – that the key word is **wandering**. Not so: the key word is **management**. If you read their anecdotes, or think of the good MBWA managers you know, you see that their secret is that in wandering around they spot things that need fixing and get them fixed fast. By wandering around they are taking a micrometer slice through the organisation to see what's happening – particularly the sub-critical problems which have yet to develop into a real issue. By getting them fixed fast they are sending a message to the rest of the troops that the boss hasn't relinquished interest just because he has relinquished some controls.

One stationmaster in the old days talked about how he used to run King's Cross. 'When I first went there I took a notebook and on each page I wrote the name of a location or a function under my command. Three or four times a day, or when I didn't have anything to do, I would open the notebook randomly and go and take a look at whatever it directed me to. I soon get the reputation for being everywhere, though I probably spent less time in total on station inspection.'

There are good scientific precedents for this style. Years ago, the behaviorist B. F. Skinner studied the behaviur of rats and other animals when put into cages in which food was delivered in small amounts when the rat pressed a lever. After establishing the connection in the rat's mind between pressing the lever and getting food, Skinner went on to experiment with different 'reinforcement schedules', i.e. he stopped rewarding every lever-pressing and looked for the ideal intervals between rewards – ideal in the sense that they would get the rat to work energetically and consistently at the lever. He tried **frequently schedules**, e.g. rewarding every five or ten presses; and **interval schedules**, e.g. rewarding every five or ten seconds. Then he tried schedules in which the intervals were randomised to give an average frequently or interval over a period of time; and he found that if you want to keep the rat busy at its lever, the best schedule is a **variable frequency schedule**, sometimes rewarding after two presses, sometimes after as long as twenty, but on average rewarding every ten. Manufacturers of one-armed bandits know this well; they know how to reward human beings on a variable frequency schedule just enough to keep them busy at their levers.

Unless you are going to control everything – and pay the price in initiative for so doing – the micrometer slice, the management by wandering around, on a variable frequency schedule is actually the most cost-effective way of keeping standards up.

7. The system places responsibility, authority, and information as close as possible to the people who need it in order to serve the customer. By this we don't mean the extra 5 per cent which the double-glazing salesman says he may have authority to take off your invoice if you agree to sign now. Nor do we mean being content with giving your salespeople or your customer service people the authority to give refunds on returned goods or make other small departures from established procedures. We mean giving people the responsibility, authority, and information necessary to do at least 80 per cent of their jobs without having to refer upwards for knowledge or guidance, including the freedom sometimes not to do the job in the established and traditional way if this will mean a better service. In the ideal situation, a customer should only have to make two phone calls to find out what he needs to know or to get what he wants; one to your switchboard, and one to the person the switchboard directs him to.

DESIGNING EFFICIENT SYSTEMS

8. The designers of the system begin by considering how it should reflect and affect the aims of the organisation. Only then do they go on to consider matters of form design, participation, etc. You can see this at its clearest when organisations are designing systems like performance appraisal, Management by Objectives, etc. They usually start and finish with the design of a form. They don't ask themselves whether they want the system to be primarily concerned with spotting poor performance, improving current standards, or developing managers for the future. They don't ask whether they want the system to allow or discourage risk-taking; to respond quickly or slowly; to be a 'telling' system or a 'listening' system. They don't ask about who should own the system. So they get a pretty little form which is out of sympathy with the way most people do their jobs, and the form is ignored or filled in with little commitment and to no purpose.

9. The designers of the system pilot it before introducing it throughout the organisation, if this is at all possible. This is common sense. What people often forget is that the purpose of a pilot is to see where the faults and problems are; the purpose is not to get it right first time, though this is a pleasant bonus if it happens. Many people opt out of the pilot stage for fear of losing face if they are publicly exposed as having not thought of everything and as having to back-track; so they install the system company-wide, and then find themselves forced into making course corrections as the inevitable faults become apparent. Or they go through the motions of a pilot stage, but don't bother to collect the evidence about how well it is working. British Telecom now have all their Directory Enquiries computerised. In its early days Valerie Stewart got a letter from a potential client, with whom she has since done a lot of business, asking her to contact them – they'd tried to find her phone number, having the correct address, and had been told firmly that she was ex-directory. An odd thing for a fee-earning consultant. She rang British Telecom, who denied that such a thing was possible. Protests that she had better things to do with her time than make non-existent complaints were ignored. Two years later, trying to track down another commercial organisation, she was told that they were ex-directory. She rang the publishing firm which had printed the Managing Director's latest book, got the number, and phoned them. They weren't ex-directory either.

A good pilot is something you learn from, not something you do for practice for the big system.

10. The system is designed to follow the natural rhythms and seasons of the business rather than to impose its own timing. A retailing firm is taken over by a conglomerate. In the conglomerate, budgets are prepared during the last three months of the year. So, says the new Head Office, that's when you'll be preparing your budgets too. What about the Christmas trade, and the January Sales, say the managers of the retailing firm. Budgets are very important, says Head Office. Professional administrators come into the National Health Service. Being administrators, they have meetings. They have meetings in the afternoon, which is when the doctors do their out-patients clinics. Do I go to the meeting and leave my patients, asks the consultant, or do I attend to my patients and find that half my ultra-sterile highly specialised eye hospital is going to be taken over by dental patients in my absence?

BYPASSING THE SYSTEM

11. The system is geared up to respond quickly, or be bypassed, when there is urgent need. We have already said that busting the bureaucracy does not mean abandoning all systems and controls. There will be a time when even the existing minimalist systems and controls need to be questioned or bypassed because an unforeseen situation has happened and a quick response is necessary because otherwise the customer will go elsewhere, or production will be lost, or a valuable employee go to the competition. Nowadays the bit of the system which most often needs to be bypassed is the computer, because it imposes its own rigidities which people seem to think have the force of law. 'I ordered a really rather beautiful car. It was my present to myself for doing well. It was the only bright spot in an otherwise dull and dismal life. I planned the colour scheme exactly the way I wanted it. Then I went down to the garage to take my existing car in for servicing. While I was there the salesman came in with a long face. Bad news, he said. They're not making the colour you want any more; they phoned up on Friday and gave us an hour and a half to choose a new one, so we chose Stone. Is that all right? No, it's not, I said. If I can't have the colour I originally wanted then my second choice is blue. You can't change it now, says the salesman, it's in the computer. They haven't painted the bloody thing yet, have they, I said, and even if they have, I'm not buying a Model T Ford. So he gave me the name of the customer services person at Head Office. She'd obviously been on a customer awareness training course, because she was very sympathetic, but basically she was getting me ready to receive the answer No. Which I wasn't prepared to have. So I gave her four hours, and then phoned the Managing Director and gave him some free medical advice, and would you believe he phoned back the following day and said that it was coming in the colour I wanted. But it took me about four hours in all, which I haven't got.' There are two lessons in here: the first, how easy it is for manufacturing and production people to lose contact with the impact of their decisions on the customer; the second, how difficult it was to by-pass the system once it had locked into a particular mode.

12. The designers or owners of the system have built in a procedure for monitoring how people react to it and whether it continues to meet the needs for which it is designed. A badly-received system, or one that has become obsolete, is changed

without fuss. Yesterday's success formula is not necessarily what you want tomorrow; yes, it was useful, yes, it was well-managed, but no, it is now out of date. We see this perhaps most clearly in organisations that claim a superordinate reason for existence: politics, parts of the military and of the established church. Mountbatten's attempts to get all three services to co-operate taxed even his persuasive genius. Women have never been priests in the Church of England, and that is good enough reason for them never to be so in the future. This country has never had proportional representation; local councillors have never been paid a salary; the National Health Service has always been free on point of receipt, so this is how it shall be for ever.

There is a story about a relatively senior man in the Pentagon. As an experiment, he was given an office, two staff, and a budget, but not given any kind of job description. Within two years this man without a mission had indented for more office space; taken seven people onto his staff; and significantly increased his budget. And how many committees do you know which have voluntarily disbanded themselves, pronouncing their purpose completed?

There is no shame in scrapping a system if it has achieved its purpose and now needs to disappear. Unfortunately, in a bureaucracy it can be difficult to measure the contribution of a particular individual or function; so the only measure of one's worth is often the size of budget or the number of staff one controls. Giving up one's power base because its purpose is no longer valid is very difficult; more so when the people around you are playing the same game.

13. When the system needs to be bypassed, the onus of proof is on the owner of the system rather than on the person wanting to bypass it. In other words, people should be free to behave with authority until they are stopped for a reasonable purpose. They should not have to ask permission to do something new. The group in ScotRail who commandeered the Inter-City 125 to start from Elgin did the planning first and presented it as almost a *fait accompli* – it is difficult to run your own private trains over the BR metals. Their attitude: 'This is what we propose to do; this is why' this is how much business we can gain; we'd like to start on Money,' is much preferable to the style that has people jumping up and down asking 'Please may I . . .?' about everything they want to do.

14. The system does not automatically stop people from taking risks or making experiments, and does not demand proof in advance that experiments will be successful. Fisons Pharmaceuticals is now one of the most profitable parts of the business. Years ago, a senior researcher discovered a drug which he thought would be useful in the treatment of asthma. He put some development effort into it. Eventually he was told to stop; the proposition looked too risky. Instead of stopping, he went underground, siphoning money from other budgets to keep his special project going. Later, when the company was in severe difficulties and had few new products to offer the market, he produced his baby, now further developed. That drug is now known as Intal; it is one of the biggest aids to asthma sufferers, and a major contributor to Fisons group profits.

The point of this story is that the researcher was senior enough to conceal the activities, and had the positional power which enabled him to be 'economical with the truth' to his bosses.

Another story: there is a women's magazine, on both sides of the Atlantic, called *Cosmopolitan.* The story goes that the editor of the US magazine called together her staff and told them, in confidence, that they would soon be starting a new magazine. It would appeal to the young, educated, liberal, free-thinking woman. She asked for ideas about the kind of features and articles it should carry, the advertisers who should be approached, the best marketing strategies, etc. She was deluged with ideas. Several days later she came back to the same group. 'Got news for you,' she said. 'There isn't going to be another magazine; we already have one which appeals to the young, educated, liberal, free-thinking woman. What I want to know is – what stopped you all from putting these wonderful ideas on my desk weeks ago?'

How many *Cosmopolitan* or Intal stories are there in your organisation?

PERSONNEL SYSTEMS

15. A system that is primarily designed to promote dialogue between people should not be changed into one whose main purpose is to generate information for purposes of record-keeping and/or planning. Personnel systems are particularly but not exclusively vulnerable to this complain. It's a good idea for the boss and subordinate to talk to each other, so let's have a

performance appraisal system. The system is duly designed and installed. Then lots of other people get in on the act; the salary planning people realise that assessments of performance are made at performance appraisal interviews, so they demand access in order to do their salary planning. The manpower planning people realise that assessments of potential, and career aspirations, can be collected similarly. The training people use it to gather training needs. And so on, until the original purpose is long forgotten and the two people for whom the system was started – boss and subordinate – feel that they have no say in the process whatsoever.

Thus, enabling systems. You need them to bust your bureaucracy. The perception and the will are useless without the vision of what the future could be like without the constraints of a corset. It is no good just throwing off existing systems – even if you could; they have remarkable persistence – without having something to replace them with. An empowering system, one which encourages people to give their best rather than assuming that left alone they will seek to do their worst, will take you through into the integrated phase.

One final word on busting the bureaucracy. To do it on any scale, you need to be a senior manager or have the guardianship of a senior manager. But if you are a senior manager in the firm in the systems crisis, you may be isolated from the people who can tell you best how the organisation needs to change. Those people are further down the organisation, and the customers. Don't lose touch with them. Come in to work on a Saturday morning, or the night shift. Eat in the staff canteen. Go on a staff training course and go down the pub with them. Pretend you're a customer, and go into one of your outlets, or ring yourself up from a distant location. See what you learn. Then build a developing organisation, and keep in touch with the grass roots.

15 · Teamwork

We said in the first part of this book that part of the reason for ScotRail's success lies in the teamwork that went throughout the organisation from top to bottom. How do you get that teamwork to work for you?

We used the Myers-Briggs/Jungian typology to describe the ScotRail team: the four differentiations between extraversion and introversion, sensing and inuition, thinking-judgement and feeling-judgement, and the use of the judging or perceptive process in the external world. It is a useful typology not merely because it is true, but because it is simple and easy for the lay person to understand, and we shall use it in this chapter as a way of describing the conflicts and complementarities which can arise in a team.

INTERACTION WITHIN INDUSTRY

Where there is a difference in MBTI type, there is opportunity for conflict, or for complementarity, depending on how much insight the parties concerned have into their differences and the use they are disposed to make of them.

The most severe conflicts within industry tend to occur across the S–N and the J–P boundaries, and they can look like this:

N; Why don't we . .
S: It's been done already.

N: I wonder what would happen if . . .
S: Please stick to the facts.

N: I have a theory that . . .
S: Stop theorising while there's work to be done.

N: Can we paint a scenario . . .
S: Can we approach this one step at a time?

N: I've finished now.
S: Oh no you haven't . . .

and . . .

S: We need to look at the fine print . . .
N: Don't bother me with the details.

S: I've drawn up a critical path analysis . . .
N: I'll give it a quick glance.

S: We cannot possibly take on any more work now.
N: I said we'd manage somehow.

S: You asked for the Bring Forward file . . .
N: Leave it while I get on with planning tomorrow.

S: If it doesn't work, look at the instructions.
N: If it doesn't work, kick/shake/poke at it.

The **sensing** type in these interactions in showing all the typical behaviours which annoy the intuitive type: the preference for facts rather than fantasies, the careful attention to detail, the memory for precedent, the preference for planning one step at a time, the dislike of inspiration. And the **intuitive** is showing all the typical behaviours which annoy the sensing type: the preference for tomorrow rather thah yesterday, and ability to dream, the preference for the big picture rather than the details, the willingness to follow inspiration no matter where it may lead.

And some illustrations across the J/P boundary:

J: Let's get this show on the road.
P: What's the hurry?

J: I'd like us to set some objectives . . .
P: What I do is my own affair, even if you are paying me.

J: I'm the boss . . .
P: That's your problem.

J: Deadline!
P: What deadline?

J: I didn't get where I am today without hard work, effort, following the rules . . .
P: I didn't get where I am today without enjoying myself, having a good time, seeing everything . . .

and . . .

P: I tell you the situation's different . . .
J: We made a plan and we'll stick to it.

P: There's a lot going on here . . .
J: Just stick to the essentials.

P: This is not a battle we can win.
J: We'd best call up some more resources, then.

P: I'm not going to sell my soul just for your idea of success.
J: But you must play the game by the rules.

P: We can leave this, we don't have to decide yet.
J: We have to take a decision.

The **judging** type here is showing all the behaviours which annoy the perceptive type: the preference for plans and structure, order and deadlines; the unwillingness to alter the plan once made; the respect for hierarchy, rules, and authority. And the **perceptive** type is showing all the behaviours which annoy the judging type: the openness to new information which can look like fickleness; the dislike of hierarchy and authority; the preference for leaving things until the last minute; the resistance to having objectives imposed.

There are usually, in industry, fewer open conflicts across the two other boundaries, but their potential existence should not be ignored. Extraverts and introverts can clash: the introvert's need for silence can interfere with the extravert's need for noise and bustle; the introvert's characteristic pause for reflection can annoy the extravert who wants to get on with it; the extravert's need for variety can appear strange to the introvert who is content to work for a long time on a project. However, the open conflict arises less often than with the other two distinctions simply because the introvert takes a lot of goading before he will tell the extravert to please go away; the introvert's preferred world in his inner world, and for him to engage in conflict with the extravert means that he has to come into his less preferred world.

And there are fewer open conflicts across the T/F boundary for two reasons: one is that thinking types outnumber feeling types in huge proportion in most organisations, so that the opportunity for conflict is less common; and while strong thinking types tend to relate best to other thinking types, feeling types have the ability to relate well to most people. So the potential T/F conflict is usually averted by the feeling type backing down, creating harmony, finding ways of avoiding argument. The feeling type will stand his ground when a value he holds highly is violated, however; few things are more surprising than the sight of an INFP – typically the ones who feel the most and reveal the least – taking a strong stand against a practice he regards as morally wrong.

It might help if we had one or two real-life examples of conflict at work or in the home, illustrated through type theory:

In a family group, Dad was an ENTJ, all the scores very strong. Mum was an INTJ, but all the scores weak. Daughter was an ENFP, all the scores strong; son an ESTJ, scores medium. The major conflict was between mum and daughter. As an INTJ, mum has the potential to be determined, driven to mastery, confident of the rightness of her opinions, and creative; but her scores are fairly weak, and she has never had the chance to fully develop her preferences. Daughter as an ENFP has an incredibly effortless ability to get on with people; a strong preference for leaving things until the last minute; resistance to authority (including mum's and school's); and a talent for happiness and popularity. So mum would nag the daughter to get on, achieve, do things on time, spend less time at parties, be more choosy about her friends. And she would be almost jealous of her daughter's ability to navigate effortlessly in a world of people – the INTJ prefers the world of ideas. If you add to this the fact that mum's N score is swamped by dad's much greater N score, then you see that mum is being driven to work out of her weaker side: someone in a partnership has to do all the S things like ordering the provisions, seeing that the bills are paid, taking care of repairs to the house. Mum's N score is not as great as dad's, but she would welcome the chance to use it. And the ESTJ son say happily playing with his computer and wondering what all the fuss was about.

COUNSELLING

Part of the answer was some counselling for all parties, based on trying to get them to value the differences amongst them rather than resenting them; and mum started to find opportunities to exercise her INTJ-ness, by taking up lots of creative pursuits which would feed her dominant but undeveloped N-score.

Another example of conflict is to be found in the ENTJ director who was working for an ISTJ boss. This is not an uncommon pairing, given the changes that are happening in many organisations. It is difficult for an ENTJ not to want to change things; it is hard for an ISTJ to see the need for change. The ENTJ looks to the future, and hhe ISTJ looks to the past and to precedent. The ISTJ is inclined to believe that promotion should be on the basis of seniority; the ENTJ to believe that it should be on the basis of achievement. The ENTJ has the natural leadership qualities common to many ENTJ's; the ISTJ resents this. The ISTJ asks for plans to be set out clearly, one step at a time; the ENTJ plans by leaping towards his goal and then working out the force-field that will influence his path. The ISTJ sets up systems and procedures, and the ENTJ treats them cavalierly. The ENTJ moves fast, and forgets some details; the ISTJ moves methodically, and never forgets detail. They don't get one.

Where there are differences, there can be conflict, as we have seen. Or the parties concerned can come to value the different perspectives, the wider range of alternatives, that their differences offer them. Put very simply:

INTUITIVES NEED A SENSING TYPE

To bring up pertinent facts which the intuitive may have missed in his haste to look towards the next thing that needs doing.

To remember details that may have been missed, particularly the details that might not have appeared to be relevant at the time. A sensing type's ability to revisit the 'scene of the crime' and recall things that the intuitive did not notice can be very useful.

To read the small print. Typically an intuitive will skip-read, looking for the things that stand out on first inspection, but not go over the document with a fine tooth-comb. Watching an intuitive getting to grips with a new piece of machinery, or trying to fixe a fault, can be quite amusing; if they are true to type, the last thing they do is read the instruction book.

To check records, read proofs, do arithmetic. Most intuitives who have to work with detail have developed a way of overcoming what they know is an innate ability to skip over decimal points, participles, and connecting words.

To notice what ought to be attended to. When Valerie Stewart, who has virtually no S score at all, was proof-reading her first book, she remembers vaguely sniffing the air and thinking: 'Funny time for someone to have a bonfire.' Then she noticed that it was a bit noisy outside. When the commotion eventually penetrated, she went out to find a 14-brigade forest fire raging in the 10 square miles of woodland on the other side of the road from her house.

To keep track of the details. Most intuitives, unless they have learned to discipline themselves out of it, would have a filling system that used every available bit of horizontal space and was totally impenetrable to a sensing type – or to another intuitive unless they had a similar pattern to their internal melee. Sensing types have a good memory and are usually neat and tidy.

To have patience. Intuitives are driven by a need to get on with shaping tomorrow. They can abandon today's task – not because it is difficult or complicated, but because it is boring. A good sensing type has the patience to work through the boring bits.

SENSING TYPES NEED AN INTUITIVE

To see the possibilities in a situation. The intuitive wants to change, re-shape, ask 'what if' questions. The sensing type left alone may be content to take things as they are. If you really want to run a good brain-stroming session, separate the sensing and the intuitive types; give the task of producing something new to the intuitives, and give it to the sensing types to make it real and workable.

To bring ingenuity to problem-solving. Think of Kekule, sitting by his fire, wondering why aromatic carbon compounds had the composition they did when none of the existing ways of mapping the relationship of carbon atoms accounted for the relative proportions of the different elements; then he has a great Aha! moment and thinks of the benzene ring. There is no way that this inspiration can be built up one step at a time; it takes the ingenuity of the intuitive thinker to re-arrange the universe.

To be unafraid of complexity. Sensing types can remember any number of facts, but are less good at remembering patterns and complexities. This leads them sometimes to over-simplify a complex situation in order to have something they can understand more easily. The intuitive may have difficulty remembering the details, but they have an ability to comprehend relationships which makes them invaluable in complex situations.

To explain what another intuitive is talking about. Because sensing types get their data through their five senses, and people's senses operate in pretty much the same way in different people, you usually find that sensing types have little trouble agreeing on the data that matter to them. It is different with intuitives. The language in which they do their important thinking is metaphorical, private (especially with introverted intuitives), and less penetrable not merely to a sensing type but maybe also to another intuitive who does not share the first one's metaphorical framework: some people's imagery is visual, some verbal, some musical, some mechanical, some kinaesthetic. This leads to communication problems between intuitives (if you are an intuitive, can you recall the wonderful feeling of finding a fellow-intuitive who shares your metaphorical framework, a feeling of not having to drive on the brakes, which leads up an instant spiral of friendship) but even more between intuitives and sensing types. Given that sensing people outnumber intuitives three to one in the general population, it's no wonder that the intuitives sometimes need someone to speak for them.

To look far ahead. If they each only had ten minutes to spare, the average intuitive would rather start something new and the average sensing type would rather finish something off. The resting thoughts of an intuitive are aabout the future (not always optimistically, by the way). The sensing type's preoccupation with the here and now needs to be balanced by the intuitive's ability to look weeks or months or years or decades ahead.

To furnish new ideas. Most entrepreneurs are intuitives. Sensing types are good at solving problems through applying past experience; intuitive types are often happiest working in the 'unknown solutions to unknown problems' box.

To be unafraid of things that look impossible. 'Most men look at things as they are, and ask Why? I look at things as they could be, and ask Why Not?' That is the kind of statement more likely to come from, and appeal to, an intuitive.

FEELING TYPES NEED A THINKING TYPE

To analyse. The thinking type's respect for logic, perception of cause and effect, sense of priorities, does not come naturally to the feeling type. They are more likely to want to cure the pain, or to raise people's morale, and this can lead to expediency or wasted resources.

To organize. Again it is the thinking type's respect for logic which leads them to be a good organiser, particularly a -TJ type.

The find the flaws in advance. Feeling types have a preference for harmony, and often don't like getting or giving bad news. So to look at a proposal and see what might be wrong with it does not come naturally to a feeling type, and they are less likely than a thinking type to risk offending people by pointing out that something is unlikely to work as proposed.

To reform what needs reforming. Often it is the feeling type who sees the need for reform (and we mean reform rather than reorganise) but they need a thinking type around to actually carry out the reformation. A Gandhi needs a Nehru; Jesus called Matthew the tax-gatherer out of his tree to come and serve him; maybe one reason why the Peace People failed in Northern Ireland was that their feeling-vision was never really supported by some thinking-judgement to put it into practice.

To weigh the law and the evidence. The feeling type understands mercy and the thinking type understands justice. Sometimes one is appropriate, sometimes the other. The thinking type is a useful balance to the feeling type's leaning towards mercy even where it would be inappropriate. Take for instance the case of a strong feeling type running an organisation who knows that unless some people are made redundant now the whole organisation will go bankrupt in a few months. This is a relatively easy decision for the thinking type to take: the evidence points to some redundancies now, and so that is the course of action to be taken. Left alone, the feeling type may agonise about the decision for so long that the feared bankruptcy does in fact materialise.

To hold consistently to a policy. In the case of the organisation having to shed labour, there would always be a danger that the feeling type, having made the decision, would then go back on it for special cases: 'We can't let Mary go, she's supporting an elderly mother . . . nor can we let Jim go even if he's only been here six months, because he was out of work for two years before . . . and poor Fred's nearly 52, he'll never get another job with his lack of qualifications . . .'. The thinking type is much more likely to take the decision and stick with it.

To stand firm against the opposition. Feeling types are more sensitive to pain and threat. When they have to stand up against opposition, it costs them. An extraverted type will show it; an introverted type is less likely to wear his distress on his sleeve, but it's there all right. The thinking type is more likely to be able to tough it out without it costing so much.

THINKING TYPES NEED A FEELING TYPE

To persuade. There is a senior manager in an organisation which he fears is not going to survive. He has commissioned studies, and written papers for the Board, on what he sees as the most likely alternative paths the company could take. They are very good papers, and they get ignored; because the one thing he has left out of his calculations is that he has forgotten to think about the Board's feelings. His papers do not make them hurt enough to want a solution. They take little account of the fact that it is difficult to lose face and de-commit from a course of action you have followed for the past five years. He is under the common misapprehension that logic wins arguments; and that winning the argument with someone is the same thing as persuading them to change their behaviour. Not surprisingly, he has a strong T score. He needs a feeling type to help him work through the issues of getting the Board to want a solution; he needs a feeling type to help him realise that this is indeed an important issue in its own right.

To conciliate. The thinking style is more likely to settle arguments on the basis of whoever is the stronger wins. Robert Kennedy's book on the Cuba crisis, *13 Days,* shows very clearly how thinking-judgement and feeling-judgement combined to produce a good solution: 'Always leave the other guy a bridge. Always give him an opportunity to back down without losing face. Never leave him in a position where he feels he has no alternative than to fight.'

To forecast how others will feel. There is a good example of this in George Orwell's *The Road to Wigan Pier,* when he discusses the effect of unemployment on people's consumption patterns. Someone had worked out that you could feed a family for about ninepence a week, provided that you and they were satisfied with porridge and turnips; Orwell points out that in fact if you've no job and nothing to do then you need a bit of fun, a bit of stimulation. How many times does one hear the strong thinking type arguing that people 'ought to see the sense' in what he proposes, and the feeling type saying that no matter how sensible, they won't? How many public policies have been based on the assumption that people will logically leave their homes and their roots and go where the work is; will read the statistics about taking too much drink or drugs and stop; will understand the figures about nuclear power, or fluoridation, or vaccination, and be appeased? It takes a feeling type to understand that fears and hopes which are not based on data are nonetheless real.

To arouse enthusiasm. In a group of assorted people, it's usually the feeling types who are the custodians of the group's morale. Two weeks or two years after the event, you can ask them how so-and-so was feeling at any particular time and they can tell you. Most comedians are strong feeling types, and no wonder (hence the legend of the sad clown). A thinking type works on preferences; a feeling type understands enthusiasms.

To teach, particularly to teach those who don't want to be taught. If you look at the MBTI profiles of professional teachers, you find that young children are taught by SJ's (who are primarily interested in control) or NF's (who are interested in people's development). Academic subjects are more often taught by NT's. (By the way, 35 per cent of our children are SP's, and most unlikely to meet a teacher of similar temperament during their schooling. Here perhaps is one reason why SP's typically are under-achievers at school and tend to go back into education late, if at all). An NT teacher teaches physics; an NF teacher teaches children.

To sell. Because of the understanding of other people's emotions and feelings, feeling types often make better salespeople than thinking types. The kind of selling where one expert meets another and the 'sale' is in fact a comparison of data is done well by the thinking type; but the persuasive selling, the kind of sale where you have to look after the prospect's morale and feelings as well as the facts, is often done best by the feeling type.

To appreciate the thinker. The thinking style, particularly in business, is a very macho phenomenon. It is difficult for the thinking type to admit to other like-minded colleagues that he's feeling depressed, or angry, or happy. A feeling type can act like a kind of lightning conductor, making it OK for his colleagues to talk about how they feel. Most of us, if we're lucky, have a feeling type friend who picks up the phone to talk just at the right time, or sends a supportive note, or takes us down the pub and makes it possible to talk.

JUDGING TYPES NEED A PERCEPTIVE TYPE

To see that the plans need to change. The judging type works best when he can plan his work and work to the plan. This sometimes leads to the plan taking priority over the data. If any of the senior officers responsible for the Charge of the Light Brigade had had a perceptive ADC working with them with enough clout to get their chief to listen, 550 poor souls would not have charged into the Russian guns. Lord Raglan formed a plan without being able to see the battlefield; and the rest just passed it on, without seeing the need to suggest that the plan be changed since it was patently formed on inadequate data.

To be rebellious to silly rules. The judging type is happy with structure, authority, and hierarchy. They respect rules, because they got where they were by hard work and obedience to the rules. They'll stop at a red light at four o'clock on a summer morning in a country town where it's obvious that not even the birds are up and about yet. It takes a perceptive type wo ask the question: 'Is this rule really necessary, and do we have to obey it?'

To stop them getting off the mark too quickly. Another feature of judging types is that they are anxious to get started. They set sail, and then wonder what course to take: literally, in some cases – Henry Ford chartered a 'Peace Ship' with which he was to put an end to the First World, had it provisioned, set course for Europe, and then was faced rather too late with the question of why was he going there and what was he going to do once he had arrived. A perceptive type will ask the question: 'Is this a decision we need to take now? Can we anything by postponing action?' The King of Hearts – sentence first, verdict afterwards – was almost certainly a judging type.

To point out that other matters ought to take priority. Judging types, once set on a course, are difficult to deflect. To plan, the D-day landings took lots of thinking-judgment; once on the beaches, a few perceptive types were necessary to make the quick adaptations to the plans required by the enemy bombardment.

To encourage the judging type to have fun. Perceptive types, particularly sensing perceptives, have an enormous capacity for sheer fun and *joie de vivre*. Many judging types find it difficult to be totally, inconsequentially, light-heartedly relaxed. The court jester who pricked the King's pomposity and waved his pig's bladder at the royal chamberlain was almost certainly a perceptive type.

PERCEPTIVE TYPES NEED A JUDGING TYPE

To stick to the plan. Judging types are good at planning, and at sticking to the plan once made. Perceptive types would rather stay spontaneous, and see what comes up. This can lead them to going down all sorts of interesting byways rather than doing what they said they would do. 'I can't start the report because I've run out of paper, and that means I have to go to the shop to get some more, and that means getting the car out, but I ought to clean the windscreen, and I ought to wash the chamois leather first, which means taking the hyacinth bulbs out of the bucket, so I ought to put them into their peat bowls, which means finding the peat . . .'

To encourage conformity to sensible rules. There are clear differences in the early upbringing of many judging and perceptive types. Judging types tend to come from backgrounds where the success formula was clear and consistent – you were promised a bicycle if you passed the 11+, and when you passed you one. So judging types grow up trusting in rules and authority, because they have seen it work for them. Perceptive types, by contrast, tend to come from backgrounds where the authority figures were absent or contraditory: where Dad said one thing and Mum another, where the school standards conflicted with home standards, where one or other parent was absent. Thus perceptive types grow up believing that the grown-ups have this game called Success, and they won't let me play. They learn to distrust rules and authority, and will often break the rules for no reason other than the fact that rules, for them, are there to be broken. A sensible judging type can make clear the difference between arbitrary rules and sensible rules; and if he or she is really sensible will do this in a way that makes the rules look less like the whim of some distrusted authority figure.

To make the hierarchy work. Perceptive types tend to be distrustful of authority and dismissive of hierarchy. Talented perceptive types very often do not survive into the higher reaches of organisations, at least in part because their attitude may not be respectful enough. In the IBM Scientific Centre at Peterlee, many years ago, Colin Bell the Director said that his job was to act as an umbrella over his people to protect them from the incursions of the rest of the IBM hierarchy. In most scientists the dominant process is perceptive; Bell had it right. History is littered with examples of perceptive types who had judging types around to manage the hierarchy: Barnes Wallis, Lindemann, Leonardo; and some who didn't, like Alan Turing.

To organise. Most secretaries are ESFJ and ISFJ – managing the details and their bosses' morale. They need the sensing ability to notice the details and the judging ability to assemble the details to fit a plan. Perceptive types are typically more tolerant of waste, disorder, and general disorganisation; more likely to forget appointments, miss trains, let meetings overrun because they've got interested in the subject. A judging type supplies the required degree of planning, organising, and controlling.

To work to sensible deadlies. Most perceptive types are more likely to be rated as creative professionals than as firm managers. And it seems to be part of the deal that when you employ a creative professional you also buy yourself a great deal of nail-biting time wondering whether the material really will be delivered as promised. They are not all, thank goodness, like Dylan Thomas, who was writing the last act of *Under Milk Wood* as the first was being performed; but most perceptive types have trouble with deadlines. Their ability to go chasing after new ideas and new information, and their resistance to authority, means that when the boss chases them to get something done they are more likely to do something else than finish the task in hand. 'I went off on holiday and set him very clear objectives for the task he had to achieve,' said the harrassed manager of one wild ENTP. 'And when I came back he hadn't done a stroke on the project I set him, but had started and finished two others that interested him but which were nothing like as important or urgent.'

To set standards. We do not mean by this that a perceptive type usually has lower standards than a judging type. Either can be a perfectionist or a sloven. The operative word here is **set**. Perceptive types usually respond very badly to systems like performance appraisal and objective-setting, because of their resistance to authority. They therefore resist any attempt to have standards set for them, or to be asked to declare their own standards in advance. A sensible judging type can recognise this and will negotiate the kind of compromise which says: 'Let's agree standards for **what** you will do, and provided that you deliver I will keep out of setting standards about **how** you do it.'

We have said nothing about the complementarity of extraverts and introverts. There is a reason for this. The well-adjusted introvert has to learn to live in the outside world, although it his not his preferred world. And the extravert had from time to time to live in his less preferred world of ideas. In any team composed of a mix of the two, therefore, some people will be working in their most preferred world and some in their least. The keys to harmony in the group lie in a good mix of tasks on the agenda: some hard concentrated work on ideas for the introverts, and some variety and action and quick feedback for the extraverts. The extraverts need to understand that the introverts take longer to get to know; do not show their feelings and values easily to strangers; need some quiet spaces in a busy day. The introverts need to understand that the extraverts' need for variety does not indicate shallowness, nor is their bonhomie a false front. Eeyore was almost certainly an ISFP; Tigger was an ENTP.

One very rarely has the opportunity to put together a team from scratch, and other considerations besides personality variables play a part. So we are not advocating that you scrap your existing teams and rebuild to get a balance; though considerations of type are useful in thinking about a balancing addition to an existing team. What is very useful, and can be done with most teams, is to put them through the Myers-Briggs Type Indicator; given them feedback as a team and as individuals; and then work out the dynamics of conflict and complementarity that are likely to occur in the team. Typically, people find that they have most in common, and get on best with, people who differ from them on one or two preferences only. (There are some complicating factors in this: intuitives tend to choose like-minded intuitives for companions, for example). The object of the exercise is to have the team members make it easy for one another to work out of their stronger side; and (an important addition) to have permission to develop their weaker side as well if this is what they want to do.

A good team contains the ability to focus on the facts and the possibilities; the here and now and the future; the logic and the people; what's good and what's reasonable. It has the ability to work with the abstract and the concrete; to work in the long- and the short-term, to make plans and to change them; to do new things and to continue what has been committed to.

16 · Personnel and Training Policies

Moving into the integrated stage is partly an issue of techniques; it is also, crucially, a people issue. Without the right people, the techniques will be an expensive failure.

In this chapter we concentrate on how the personnel policies which worked for ScotRail and for other organisations in the third stage can be used to help the transition for organisations that are coming up to the integrated stage. There are four key areas: selection, training, development, and industrial relations.

PERSONNEL SELECTION

Selection of people for moves within the organisation needs to be looked at carefully. The first question to ask is whether you have deliberately or accidentally fallen into the trap of regarding the most senior applicant as the most suitable for the job. Some bureaucracies have this almost written into their constitution, and it was the logical extension of this premise which led Peter to produce his famous Principle. In other organisations it is not an explicit rule, but it is nonetheless a practice much followed. Moving into the integrated stage requires a different kind of person; you will not always find this person by going for the most suitable applicant.

Another factor to take into account is that traditional ways of specifying what you want at selection may in fact mislead you. The correct procedure for an organisation whose main task is to do more cost-effectively tomorrow what it did yesterday, when deciding what to look for in, say, a production manager, would be to look at all the existing production managers using some sort of investigative tool – interviews, psychological testing, etc. – and from this to produce a composite picture of the effective production manager. From this specification they would then go out and recruit a few more who had the key features of the composite. This practice – laudable if you want to find out what made you successful yesterday – is in fact of very little use in making the move to the integrated stage. It is nearly always worth doing some kind of study to find out what yesterday's success formula was, because then you have an idea of how much change you need to make; but it is a mistake to regard it as a criterion study which tells you what you need to go and recruit. For the same reason, job descriptions are of less use than person-specifications.

MANAGEMENT QUALITIES

It is difficult to say with certainty what the differences are between yesterday's manager and tomorrow, but here are some:

More of . . .

The ability to take risks
Concern for people
Strategic vision
Ability to accept and/or initiate change
Personal charisma (especially in senior managers)
Concern for customers
Concern for values
Innovation and creativity

Less of . . .

Need for strong central control
Need for procedures and rules
Inability to tolerate ambiguity
Dependence on yesterday's techniques
Office-bound management
Regard for protocol and status

Valerie Stewart remembers a study done some years ago in one of the major oil companies, to find out how managers regarded the qualities of other effective managers. About half the statements collected (and we got several thousand) were about the ability to manage Head Office. Just five were about relationships with the customers. That organisation is going to have to recruit some very different managers if it is going to make it into the integrated stage; and they are going to be very difficult for the rest of the organisation to live with. Selecting a new breed of manager is not enough if they are not at the same time given the support of like-minded new managers around them; it may be better, strategically, to concentrate the new blood in one or two places and let the rest of the firm learn the lessons than to spread it thin and run the risk of being irrepairably diluted by the old style. Chris Green was given an informal guarantee that the ScotRail top team would remain undisturbed, unpoached-from, until they had had the chance to make the necessary changes.

SELECTING FROM OUTSIDE THE ORGANISATION

When selecting someone from outside to join an existing team, don't assume that pinching someone from an organisation which has successfully managed the transition will automatically do the work for you. For every Michael Edwardes there a dozen Victor Paiges – people who find that the existing bureaucracy is immovable even with the best efforts of one person. Edwardes succeeded not merely because he was good, but because British Leyland were desperate; there can have been few people there who thought that the company had an undimmed rosy future had it gone on the way it was going. Where most of the people in the organisation do not share the fears that things are shortly going to get desperate, they will tend to go on in their old way.

This caution applies not merely to the appointment of people to take over ailing organisations, but to the kind of situation where a big firm decides to spawn some smaller babies and recruit an entrepreneur to manage them. The danger here is that the parent company will continue to apply the old systems and controls to the new one, thus curtailing the entrepreneur's ability to take risks, move quickly, duck and weave in and out of markets. It is galling to be asked to institute a job evaluation scheme when you don't know from one day to the next what jobs need doing; to go through an annual budgeting cycle when you want venture capital now; to be told you can only pay union rates when you need to get the best you can. Many of the big insurance firms are in this particular problem spot right now; they are trying to get into new markets, offer new services, but are constrained by the Head Office bureaucracy which stops them getting the kind of people and systems they need for their business

PERSONNEL TRAINING

Training, for organisations in the integrated stage, ought to take on a new and larger importance. About every six months or so comes yet another report saying that the UK spends less money and time on training its managers and employees than almost every other country in the developed world. This appears to be a criticism that most people are content to shrug off, relying instead on the British instinct for muddling through; or perhaps on the fact that when the Board are reviewing a series of disasters, few people would get up and admit that they happened because staff and managers were badly trained. It would be good if industry could follow the example of the military and put its best people into the training function; good, but unlikely.

Training for what? One vital ingredient in getting out of the systems crisis is a planned programme for telling people what the crisis is; how organisations get there; and what the next stage will look like. This is emphatically not the standard exhortation to work harder. It is – or should be – a planned set of briefings in which people are told about how organisations grow and change; how the crisis arise and how people respond to them; what the experience of other organisations going through the transition is; what lies ahead; and how they can play their part.

The reason why this kind of briefing is so useful is that the systems crisis can feel like just plain bad luck. Or it can be blamed on outside forced like a downturn in the economy. If you can tell people that it is predictable; that its causes are clear, it is not an accident, and that the way out is also known, then this helps them to feel a little less at the mercy of forces they do not understand. It also helps when you come to make the case for a different management style; people know that you are not casting around for any old solutions, but have a clear idea of what is necessary and why.

The briefing is necessary, but rarely sufficient. Training in other skills and attitudes is probably necessary as well. Of the many training initiatives which ScotRail has taken, perhaps the one which has made the most significant impact is the Ullswater course; so perhaps a short interlude on how to borrow the Ullswater experience would be appropriate.

To recapitulate: we used the outdoors as a training medium not because we wanted to teach outdoor skills, nor because we wanted to put people under particularly nasty forms of stress, but because in the outdoors the consequences of your actions are so much clearer and immediate. This needs to be borne firmly in mind when planning such a course: it is easy to get seduced by the appeal of the mountains and to plan a course in which helicopters zoom from the sky, people are pitched unaware off the back of boats, and abandoned hungry for hours with a bucket of fish, string, and a drawing pin.

USING THE OUTDOORS FOR MANAGEMENT TRAINING PURPOSES

You can use the outdoors for any or all of the following management training purposes: leadership training, personal development, team-building, and organisation development. In **leadership** training the typical course is designed so that each person is put in formal leadership position for at least one task, and the classroom reviews concentrate on that person's leadership style and qualities. In a **personal development** course the emphasis is on getting people to realise for themselves that they are probably capable of more than they thought they were; have more personal resources available to them; and while there is no compulsion on them to take a particular role in the team they can learn something about how they relate to other people as leaders and followers. In a **team development** exercise a working team is taken away and given tasks which concentrate on making better the existing relationships at work. In an **organisation development** exercise a significant number of people from the same organisation are given experiences which will help them make a better contribution to the organisation as a whole – a little like a team-building exercise, but whereas a team development course examines the relationships between a particular group of people who work in the same office or on the same project, an organisation development exercise tries to build a critical mass of people within the organisation who share the same skills and attitudes.

Most of our Ullswater courses have been about organisation development; we were lucky enough to have some good leaders at all levels, and the important thing was to strengthen the ties that bound everyone in a common loyalty and common understanding. Other organisations may find that they need to start with leadership development, for example, if the evidence is that there are few junior leaders who can help manage the change process.

Once you have decided the major objective of the course, you need to think about the best way of presenting the lessons you hope people will learn. The course will probably have very little formal instruction in it; outdoor training is more likely to be 'learner-reflective' than 'trainer-planned', in the sense that one provides a rich environment in which people can learn things if they choose, but does not spoon-feed them lessons to a timetable.

The agenda for the ScotRail courses was roughly: Day One is about me as a manager – do I do what I say I do? Day Two and Three move into me as a person, issues of trust and relationships and people at work. Day Four and Five about me in the organisation – how do I fit in to it, what's happening in this changing organisation, how do I take back the lessons I have learned and apply them. The Outward Bound people at Ullswater who have helped us so skilfully say that in fact a week is a little short to achieve everything that is possible, but say also that we manage it through the use of psychological testing and feedback; good reviews; and the visit of the senior manager at the end of the course.

There are lots of organisations offering outdoor training at the moment. How do you choose a good one? Perhaps the most important factor is the flexibility to listen to your objectives and put together a course to meet them, rather than forcing you into one of their existing standard designs. Another thing to remember is that the Outward Bound tradition is one of working with adolescents; they usually do this very well, but be careful that they have the flexibility to deal with adults. Adults have a different learning style; they may not take too kindly to being told to do their own washing up, leave their muddy boots at the door, and that they can't have a drink on the premises. Check that the Centre you propose to use has staff who are used to working with adults, and make a reasonable compromise between the different age groups who will use it.

You need also so agree who will be responsible for what. Are you going to use your own trainers for the management learning and the Centre staff for safety instructions; are you going to share the responsibility for management learning? are you going to leave it all to the Centre? If you leave all the management learning to the Centre then you will probably have a good personal development course, but unless the Centre is really familiar with your organisation and can speak authoritatively about it you will have less input about your own organisation.

It ought to go without saying that you can't do it all from your own resources. Outdoor pursuits have the possibility of danger;

staffing the course with a couple of your own trainers who've done a spot of abseiling and are members of their local Mountain Rescue team won'd do.

Any training course is greatly improved by proper pre- and post-course briefing, but it is essential to an outdoor course. People need to know that the course is not a test of machismo; that it does not demand extraordinary physical skills of fitness; that they will not be evaluated on their stamina. (They shouldn't be evaluated at all). The real evaluation is longer term: back in the workplace in terms of – hopefully – improved effectiveness.

You need also to decide issues like age cut-off limits; whether the course is for people with particularly high potential or for everyone; and how many you will run and at what rate. This last point is particularly important for organisation development programmes, because you often do not see any noticeable change in the organisation until a 'critical mass' of people has been through the course and there is a reasonable chance that one person in the firm picking up the phone to talk to a fellow-employee will find that he is talking to one who has also been through the experience.

If you are going to use one Centre for any length of time, it helps if you can negotiate a constant team of instructors; and it helps even more if you can take them to see your own business in operation. The Ullswater team went up to ScotRail in the driver's cab of an Inter-City Electric.

We strongly recommend that a senior manager visit the course towards the end. If you are doing team-building, then it needs to be the line boss of the team, if he is not directly participating in the course, or someone his senior but still in the direct line of command. If you agenda is organisation development, it needs to be a more senior manage than that. The objective of the visit is to discuss with the participants the lessons they have learned on the course and how to apply them, so the manager must be of sufficient seniority and decisiveness to be able to make promises and deliver on them.

Outdoor training is fashionable now. Without false modesty, we think we can say that we put together one of the better outdoor courses; and if we analyse why it is good, it is because we are very clear about what we want to achieve with it. It is expensive in time and resources, and so not to be trifled with; but the contribution it can make is probably greater than any other form of training.

DEVELOPMENT FOR A SPECIFIC JOB

Development of people for the next job and beyond is the third issue on the personnel agenda. If you have limited resources, then the hard but fair choice is to put them at the very top and the bottom of the organisation; the top because you need good people in command, and the bottom because then you can get to people before they are contaminated by the bureaucracy, and because you will get longer pay-back for your training pound. But don't leave out the middle managers altogether; our advice is to be taken literally only when resources are stretched very tight indeed.

In many ways the best form of development is self-development, but people have to know what they are developing towards. In ScotRail we had self-development classes in which the agenda was largely suggested by the Personnel Department with line management support, but the question of who attended was left to individual people.

However, one feature of organisations in the systems crisis is that they can become very regimented, with too much specialisation between departments. You can become a manager in the accounts departments without ever having got the company's mud on your boots or talked to a customer, and you can work on the coal-face without a clue about how the bills are sent out or the supplies ordered. Therefore one vital part of good development of potential is a programme which gives people experience, early in their careers, of the work of other departments. This must be managed in such a way that the receiving manager does not see the visitor as a spare pair of hands to be used for a few weeks or months, but as a potential manager who will be all the better in his chosen speciality if he knows more about the work of other departments and functions.

Another strategic developmental issue which ought to be addressed is the development of entrepreneurial ability in junior and middle managers. This may be done by giving them their own projects to manage; more importantly, it is done by making it clear that senior management is open to good ideas and will put some resources and training behind them. They need not be earth-shattering ideas; nor, if you make wellington boots, are we telling you that if one of the staff comes with a proposal to make tennis rackets you should automatically support it. The under-used resources which you hope your young entrepreneurs will pick up and make better are most likely going to be used in the service of your existing corporate objectives. This is what Quality Circles are about; it is one reason why the best Quality Circles are given some resources to spend, because it teaches them better than anything else about how to plan resources cost-effectively.

Variations on these two themes include the use of cross-functional task forces to deal with current or future problems. Again, the key to success here lies in making sure that the task forces are really cross-functional (and, better still, cutting across the levels in the hierarchy), and that they give the people who never meet the customer the chance to do so, and the people who never look 'back of house' the chance to go there and find out about their problems. You goal is to prevent people from being over-specialised, and to give them responsibility for resources and feedback on the way they use these resources.

In organisations which are highly specialised, like the railway, there is a lot to be learned from going to other businesses to find out how they manage; not to businesses in the same trade, but totally different ones. There can't be a branch of Marks & Spencer in Scotland that hasn't at some time entertained a visiting delegation of ScotRail managers eager to learn. ScotRail plans to host a conference of senior managers in the National Health Service to try to share some of its secrets. It should not be always a delegation of visiting senior managers; a mixed group, including some quite junior people, will do better after the first one or two exchanges.

We have covered three major items of personnel policy: selection, training, and development. There remains one further important issue: that of industrial relations.

INDUSTRIAL RELATIONS

In the systems crisis, industrial relations tend to degenerate into an adversarial dialogue conducted by specialists on both sides: the Industrial Relations Manager talking to the union negotiator. Not infrequently both these parties are out of touch with the people they are their opposite number represent. The responsibility for day-to-day industrial relations is taken away from the line manager and the workforce. It is not uncommon for the senior people to be more preoccupied with finding an acceptable form of words than with solving the real problem.

It is also not uncommon for the industrial relations specialists in Head Office to get so hooked into their eleventh-hour problem-solving style than when things are quiet they go out and foment a few problems so that they can be seen to be solving them. Issues that are very important to a small number of people become issues of low priority when considered from on high. People who are not unionised – typically, professional staff and middle managers – get very little attention paid to them.

In the integrated stage, industrial relations are delegated down as far as possible to the people who own the issues. In practice, this means finding more and more ways of getting managers to communicate directly with the work-force. We have seen several examples recently – in British Leyland and the miners' strike, for instance – where management has written directly to the workers at their homes when there have been problems to resolve. It is more important, however, to think of industrial relations as an exercise in problem prevention rather than cure. Real communication, real consultation, real discussion of current issues – they have to be built into the manager's routine. Then he has the relationships ready, and hopefully some trust or at least mutual understanding established, before he needs to negotiate his way through a crisis.

There are almost certainly going to be some tough issues to resolve with the workers during the move to the integrated stage. For example, you may find yourself making people redundant from the top and middle of the organisation, but recruiting people of a different calibre to replace them. You may find yourself renegotiating the basis on which people are paid or promoted. You may have to stand firm and say that if you have delegated responsibility for industrial relations from the centre to more junior managers then this is just what you mean and there is no point trying to appeal to higher authority. You may have to train your junior managers and supervisors in better man-management skills.

In making the transition, remember:

- don't tell lies, bluster, issue threats you don't intend to fulfil.
- do remember to take into account the views and feelings of the people who have not been represented by a union.
- don't take advantage of the current rather weak position of the unions to settle old scores. Memories last a long time, and at some point you could need their help.

– judge the success of a negotiation on the implementation of the solution, not on whether or not both parties can agree on a form of words.

FLOATING SUPERVISORS

A final important word to a limited number of readers, about the 'floating supervisor' problem. This is what happens when you have a large group of workers managed collectively by a smaller group of supervisors or managers; it occurs in most industries where people work shifts. In these circumstances it is easy for the individual supervisor to duck out of standard-setting, because he knows that his fellow-supervisors do not have the same standards; easy also for the dilatory worker to play one supervisor off against another. This results in minor infractions going uncorrected, as a result of which the whole temperature of the disciplinary process becomes raised unnecessarily. If you have this situation, it is vital to reorganise so that people know that although they may report on a daily basis to a variety of supervisors, there is one particular supervisor to whom they are responsible for matters of discipline, counselling, standard-setting, and so on.

17 · Next Steps

We have tried to set out in as much detail as we can the steps which we think helped turn a dull and despairing organisation into one which is strong, alive, and going places. If you think that the ScotRail solution has anything to say to you, would you permit us a few warnings – a kind of beginner's guide to successful plagiarism?

SHARPER BUSINESS ORIENTATION

First, the commitment to a sharper business orientation, and to the development of people to fulfil the business need, has to be based on a long term strategic decision about what kind of organisation you want to run. It is not appropriate for fixing short-term cash flow problems. Short-term problems may alert you to the fact that you need to be doing things differently, but we are talking about a long-term strategy. Implementing the ScotRail solution means asking people to give up what in some cases are the habits of a lifetime. They can tell if you are making this request of them in order to gain a few months' respite, after which you propose to go back to the old bureaucracy.

Second, if you are a senior manager, be aware that the bureaucracy will shield you from the early signs of the systems crisis. Therefore you have to go and look for them. If you wait for them to come to you, then in a commercial organisation you may find that the market has started to sell your shares, and in a non-commercial organisation that your staff and customers have an ingrained habit of apathy or rebellion which will be very difficult to change.

Third, there are some things we have written about in this book which need a spot of expert help in implementing. The outdoor training, and the use of the Myers-Briggs Type Indicator in team-building and personal counselling, should not be introduced by amateurs with no previous experience.

Fourth, if yours is the kind of organisation which is subject to political control, try very hard to negotiate less political interference in the detail of the business, even though the politicians may legitimately set targets and parameters. The life-cycle of the politician is typically short, so they sometimes press for unreasonably quick results. We are talking about a long process here: don't dig up the carrots just after you've planted them to see how well they are growing.

PEOPLE

Finally, it really is about people. Have you ever seen one of those films showing speeded-up traffic going through a complicated motorway junction, and reflected on the fact that by definition about half the drivers are below average performers – and yet they still manage without too much carnage? Have you ever reflected on the fact that most people manage really quite complicated things: house purchases, income tax, job searches, problems with teenagers, stretching their budgets, falling in love . . . and by and large, most of them don't come apart under the strain? Yet as soon as they enter the doors of an organisation they somehow become disempowered: we assume that they need help to manage their time, take decisions, control their budgets? We assume that they need to be reminded to that you get more out of people if you treat them as human beings rather than ciphers. We assume that they need motivating by some outside force in order to do their best. Tony Benn once said (in a phrase that was the despair of statisticians) that 'the average person is brighter than most people think'.

We are not saying by this that people should be left alone to muddle through. This country does not spend anything like enough on training – technical, vocational, managerial. We are saying that the task of organisations going into the third stage is to build a framework in which want to do their best, and are empowered by training, by policies, by structure, and most of all by example, to give the best, and to give it with pride. We are proud to have been associated with ScotRail's success; we hope and trust that it can continue, and that the roots of its success are so firmly embedded that the inevitable storms do not tear what has been planted out of the ground. It is not a unique story; other organisations have been through similar processes. In ScotRail it is a very clearly documented story. In telling it we hope that we have been able to offer thoughts and insights which any manager can use.

Oh – and do take a train to Scotland. We'll do our best for you.

Index